Codified Leadership

Codified Leadership draws from research and evidence-based practices to provide every school leader – regardless of their experience – with authentic opportunities to improve and transform them into the very best leader. It breaks down complex leadership behaviours into manageable steps that can be used for both self and peer instructional coaching.

Exploring the real and significant challenges school leaders face every day, Section 1 considers overarching complex and nuanced leadership concepts such as trust, adaptability, clarity, and vision, providing insights into the nature and purpose of school leadership at all levels. Section 2 breaks down day-to-day tasks such as leading meetings, giving staff feedback, making decisions, and setting expectations to help leaders develop the habits and behaviours they need to lead their staff and schools effectively. Throughout, the chapters spotlight three school leaders who solve relatable problems by being deliberate and purposeful in their leadership actions.

Codified Leadership is key reading for both primary and secondary level leaders looking to promote excellence in themselves and those they work with. If you want to understand how successful leaders work – the signals they transmit, the language they speak, and the repeated actions they take – this is the ideal guide for you.

Caroline Sherwood is a Deputy Head Teacher in Devon, UK.

Andrew Finney is a Director of School Improvement, working across both primary and secondary levels in a large Multi-Academy Trust in the UK.

'In recent years there has been much debate about whether school leadership should focus on domain specific solutions to leadership conundrums or on the more generic leadership traits and skills needed for leaders to be successful. This book beautifully encompasses both, with its nuanced, evidence informed and highly practical approach. I particularly enjoyed the leadership characters whose journeys we follow throughout the book, which keep it grounded and pragmatic.

Highly recommended for leaders beginning their leadership journey or those who are just looking for an inspiring leadership top-up!'

Andy Buck,
*Founder Leadership Matters and
Creator of the BASIC Coaching Method*

'*Codified Leadership* is an invaluable resource for any leader navigating the complexities of school teams. In a field where leaders are often thrust into new situations without a roadmap, this book offers practical wisdom and actionable strategies. Drawing on a wealth of research and experience, *Codified Leadership* skillfully unpacks the nuances of vulnerability, conflict resolution, and creating a culture of trust. The emphasis on the importance of establishing predictable routines, even in the face of the unexpected, resonates deeply with the realities of school leadership.

Whether you are a seasoned headteacher or stepping into a leadership role for the first time, *Codified Leadership* provides the insights and tools to foster collaboration, navigate challenges, and ultimately, empower your team to achieve their best. This book is a must-read for anyone aspiring to lead with authenticity and create a thriving school environment.'

Ben Parnell,
CEO of a large Multi Academy Trust in the South West

'*Codified Leadership* is an enormously valuable book... full of examples from work in schools and grounded in research, this book is an important addition to the literature on school leadership.'

Mary Myatt,
Education writer and speaker

'*Codified Leadership* provides field-tested guidance and tools to help leaders accelerate progress in their schools. A timely guide for navigating complex change in a human-centred way.'

Dr Simon Breakspear,
Author Teaching Sprints, *Adjunct Senior Lecturer UNSW
(The University of New South Wales, Sydney, Australia)*

Codified Leadership

Behaviours and Habits that Make a Difference in Schools

Caroline Sherwood and Andrew Finney

Cover courtesy of Catling Creative (www.catlingcreative.com)

First published 2025
by Routledge
4 Park Square, Milton Park, Abingdon, Oxon OX14 4RN

and by Routledge
605 Third Avenue, New York, NY 10158

Routledge is an imprint of the Taylor & Francis Group, an informa business

© 2025 Caroline Sherwood and Andrew Finney

The right of Caroline Sherwood and Andrew Finney to be identified as authors of this work has been asserted in accordance with sections 77 and 78 of the Copyright, Designs and Patents Act 1988.

All rights reserved. No part of this book may be reprinted or reproduced or utilised in any form or by any electronic, mechanical, or other means, now known or hereafter invented, including photocopying and recording, or in any information storage or retrieval system, without permission in writing from the publishers.

Trademark notice: Product or corporate names may be trademarks or registered trademarks, and are used only for identification and explanation without intent to infringe.

British Library Cataloguing-in-Publication Data
A catalogue record for this book is available from the British Library

Library of Congress Cataloging-in-Publication Data
Names: Sherwood, Caroline author | Finney, Andrew author
Title: Codified leadership: behaviours and habits that make a difference in schools / Caroline Sherwood and Andrew Finney.
Description: Abingdon, Oxon; New York, NY: Routledge, 2025. | Includes bibliographical references and index.
Identifiers: LCCN 2024051959 (print) | LCCN 2024051960 (ebook) | ISBN 9781032608471 hardback | ISBN 9781032608440 paperback | ISBN 9781003460756 ebook
Subjects: LCSH: Educational leadership | Mentoring in education | Well-being
Classification: LCC LB2806 .S3545 2025 (print) | LCC LB2806 (ebook) | DDC 371.2/01—dc23/eng/20250206
LC record available at https://lccn.loc.gov/2024051959
LC ebook record available at https://lccn.loc.gov/2024051960

ISBN: 978-1-032-60847-1 (hbk)
ISBN: 978-1-032-60844-0 (pbk)
ISBN: 978-1-003-46075-6 (ebk)

DOI: 10.4324/9781003460756

Typeset in Melior
by codeMantra

Visit codifiedleadership.com for additional leadership content.
Images courtesy of Tyemedia Ltd.

Better is possible.

But it requires action.

Contents

About the authors   xi

Introduction   xii

Section 1: Floodlight leadership behaviours

1 Trust   3
2 Vulnerability   13
3 Vision   24
4 Clarity   31
5 Accountability   38
6 Adaptability   47
7 Legacy   56

Section 2: Torchlight behaviours

8 Finding your voice   65
9 Managing your team   75
10 Developing your team   82
11 Managing change   90
12 Leading Quality Assurance   97
13 Making decisions   104

14 Wellbeing	111
Conclusion	119
Our Probletunity Group	121
Sightline Presentation	122
Index	125

About the authors

Andrew Finney has dedicated 28 years to the field of education, holding two headships in England and serving on the Executive Leadership Team of a major secondary school in Brisbane, Australia. Currently, he is the Director of School Improvement in England, working across both primary and secondary levels.

With over 18 years of senior leadership experience, Andrew shares his deep passion for school leadership in this book, drawing from his extensive first-hand experience. Andrew holds a Master's Degree in Education from the University of Exeter, UK.

Caroline Sherwood has worked in education for 20 years – driven, first and foremost, by her passion for books! Caroline has extensive senior leadership experience and has a deep curiosity about human behaviour and how humans learn. Caroline is currently a deputy head in a secondary school in England, and leads teaching and learning and coaching across the secondary schools of a large multi-academy trust.

Introduction

Codified leadership

The quality of leadership is second only to teaching and learning development in improving student outcomes in schools (Robinson, 2011). It matters. We can learn from the leaders around us – both how to do it and how not to do it. Both are useful. One is, undoubtedly, more challenging to learn from. Given the recruitment challenges and the retention crisis, great leaders are more important than ever.

As a profession, we need to take more purposeful and meaningful steps towards becoming better leaders – not because we're not good enough but because we can all be even better. And better *is* possible. And it matters.

This book aims to codify leadership behaviours and habits to help us all see a clear path – a route towards being better than we were before. Because better is possible.

Our model of leadership hopes to break down something incredibly nuanced and complex into a coherent and functional tool that is adaptable to fit varying contexts (Figure 0.1).

Context

Every school's context is different. There may be some contextual factors which schools share – but often these are localised and require a different leadership response.

Contextual factors might include funding, location, community, your buildings, the characteristics of each cohort (Figure 0.2).

The sides of context are porous – meaning your school's context can change from one year to the next. What was influential and important one year may become less significant the next year.

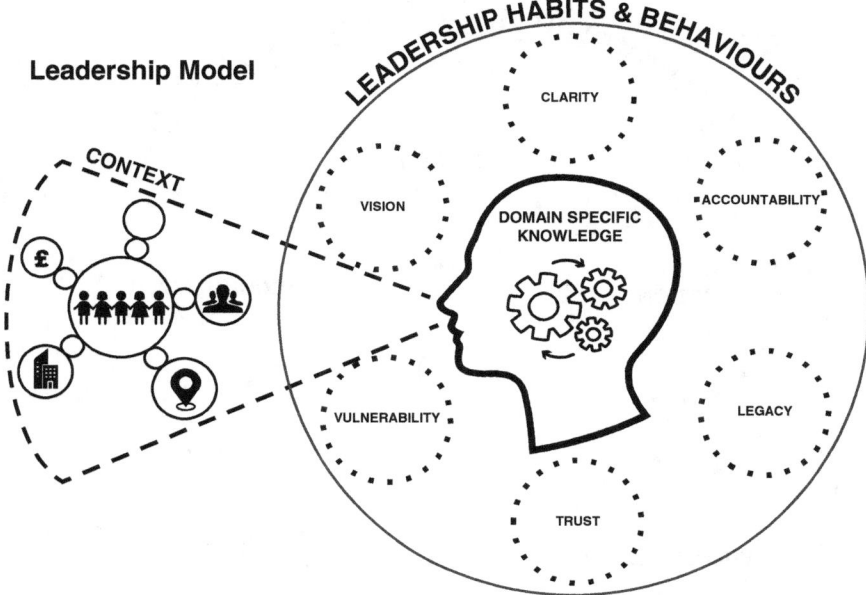

Figure 0.1 Leadership model

Figure 0.2 Leadership model – context bubbles

Behaviours and habits

These behaviours and habits are the things that the people you lead see and feel on a day-to-day basis. These behaviours are based on wide and extensive reading; they are characteristics of high-performing, successful groups – both within the world of education and beyond. These behaviours interlink – often they are very difficult to achieve in isolation (Figure 0.3).

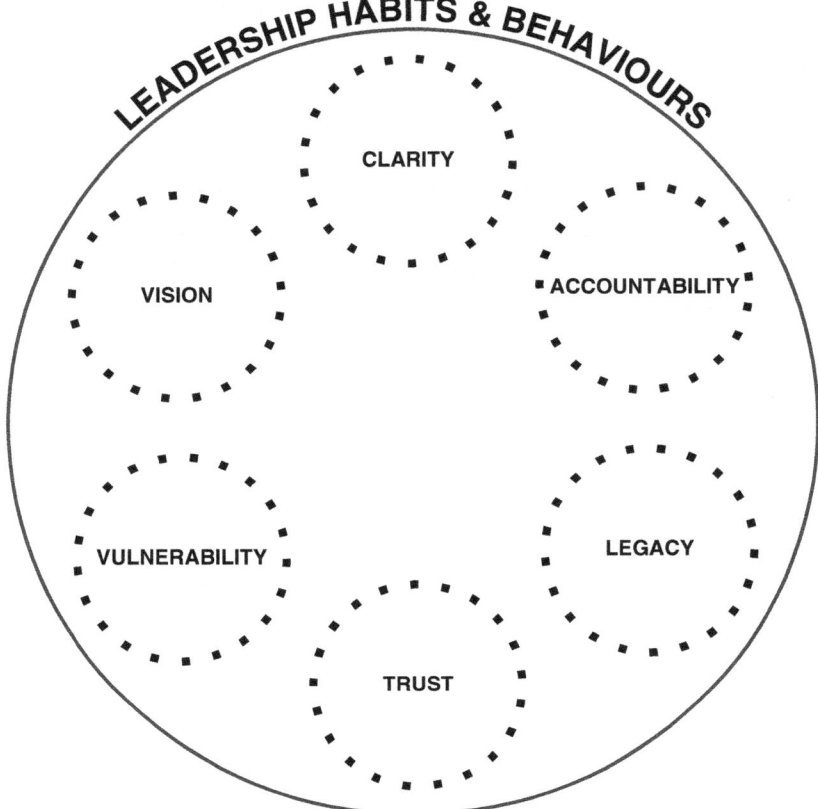

Figure 0.3 Leadership model – leadership habits

We believe, regardless of your leadership position in your school, that these big leadership behaviours and habits are the bedrock of effective leadership and team success. We explore how leaders can purposefully get better at these big behaviours and habits in this book.

Domain-specific knowledge

Domain-specific knowledge can be acquired – through deliberate action, effort, and experience. These are leadership schemas and mental models which help leaders best deal with the problems they encounter. This cog, which makes everything else possible, is about developing a deep knowledge and understanding of your area of leadership – whether that is teaching and learning, data, curriculum, teacher development. Leaders in schools might have multiple cogs working in unison – for example, a head of year might be working towards expertise in multiple domain areas: a disadvantaged cog, an outcomes cog, a behaviour cog, an attendance cog, etc. (Figure 0.4).

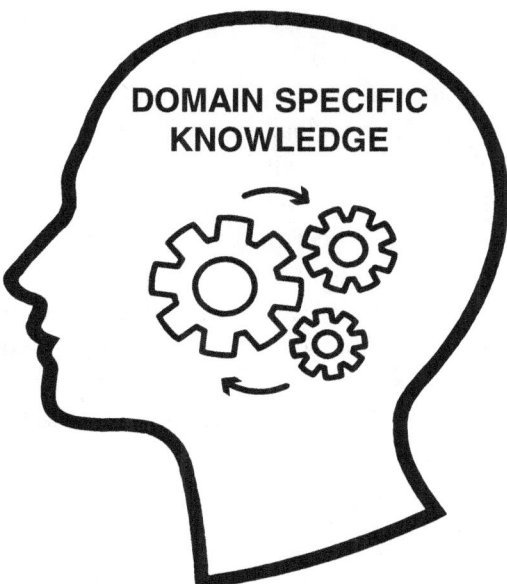

Figure 0.4 Leadership model – cog

Without appropriate domain-specific knowledge, the lens in which school leaders view their context could be flawed. Without appropriate domain-specific knowledge, the big leadership habits and behaviours could fail. It is the domain-specific cogs that facilitate the continual development and improvement of the school. We understand that domain-specific knowledge isn't static – the cogs shouldn't be motionless. It is a leader's professional responsibility to ensure they regularly engage with mechanisms that strengthen their cogs! Leaders can do this by reading and doing research, being outward-facing, and reflecting on experience. Section 2 hopes to provide leaders with the tools to keep the cogs oiled and running smoothly.

How to read this book

This book is divided into two sections – inspired by Alan Watts, a philosophy professor, who spoke metaphorically about being in a dark room – and using either a torch, or a floodlight. The torch illuminates objects in sharp relief – but is limited to one small object at a time. As you move, the object disappears, and your point of reference is lost. The floodlight illuminates the whole room – but there is a low resolution.

Section 1 explores the big, complex leadership behaviours and habits – it is the floodlight – the things the people you lead see and feel every day. This section breaks down and codifies: trust, adaptability, vulnerability, legacy, clarity, vision, and accountability. You'll think about what these habits actually look, sound, and feel like in real-life school contexts.

Section 2 aims to shine a torchlight on leadership domain expertise – the day-to-day activities leaders do and the tools they use – but often don't receive the training (or time) to do well: finding your voice; managing your team; developing your team; managing change; leading Quality Assurance; making decisions; well-being. This should help leaders enhance and use their domain-specific knowledge and expertise – it is the oil for the cog!

Throughout this book, you'll meet three school leaders who are experiencing and responding to persistent problems in schools: Elliot, Amara, and Marco. Ambition Institute (2020) identifies these persistent problems as school culture, learning and development, curriculum, behaviour, school improvement, administration, and self. These problems are universal, causal, and controllable. You will recognise their challenges and can follow the actions they take to get better than they were before. They will faithfully guide you through the chapters.

You will also read short summaries of the research from the giants on whose shoulders we stand on.

Better is possible. But it requires action

You can choose to work through this book chronologically and follow Elliot, Amara and Marco's journey in their primary and secondary school settings.

Alternatively, you could pick the sections you feel are most relevant to you – as Lencioni asks: what is most important right now?

Better yet, read this book alongside your Line Manager – or another trusted colleague; coach each other and get better than before *together*.

References

Barker, J. and Rees, T. (2020) "The persistent problems of school leadership." *Ambition Institute*, https://www.ambition.org.uk/blog/persistent-problems-school-leadership/. Accessed 3 June 2024.

Robinson, V. (2011) *Student-Centered Leadership.* Jossey-Bass.

SECTION I
Floodlight leadership behaviours

In his most recent book *Dusting off Thunderbolts*, Sir John Jones (2023) creates a beautiful link between the role of a conductor and leadership, stating that:

> like all leaders, [the conductor's] success was completely dependent on others and that, most important of all, without them he was obsolete. His power relied on making everyone around him powerful. He realised that conducting was as much about people as about music; about the heart not just the head.

Jones calls this 'The People Business'.

All people in schools – students and staff – are a leader's business, and all deserve a healthy organisation. Viewing our leadership with the floodlight on – the big picture (but nothing in sharp relief) – we can look to take purposeful steps to get better at the big, complex leadership behaviours – behaviours rooted in the people business. Like Jones says "leadership is much more than just playing the notes on the score perfectly, in the right order and in the right way" but we also need to light up the leadership arena and commit to getting better – because better is possible. And it matters.

We start by codifying the big leadership behaviours and habits. We aim to break down these huge and nuanced behaviours so that leaders can learn how to actually build and sustain the habits that make a difference in schools. Alongside this, we recognise the importance of developing tools to allow you to effectively use your domain-specific knowledge – more of this in Section 2!

Great leaders need to have *both* the domain-specific knowledge and the generic leadership behaviours to facilitate success. A great football coach may have outstanding leadership behaviours – be great at the people business – but without domain-specific knowledge about another team's tactics for example, they will ultimately become unstuck. The same is true if they have great tactics but poorly developed leadership behaviours; they will lose the changing room and ultimately be unsuccessful. We believe that school leaders should look to actively develop in both areas – they are symbiotic (Figure 1).

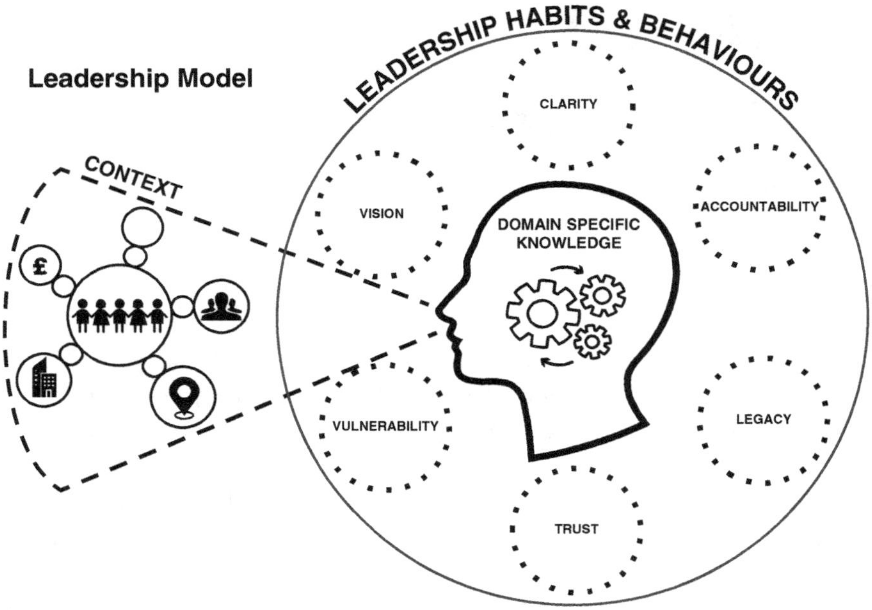

Leadership Model

Figure 1 Leadership model

For school leaders to move towards adaptive expertise, we recognise that experience is necessary but not sufficient. Great leaders will flex and adapt behaviours and habits to best fit their context and personality traits. We believe that this section gives leaders a roadmap to develop expertise in the floodlight behaviours and habits.

Reference

Jones, J. (2023) *Dusting off the Thunderbolts*. John Catt Publication.

1 Trust

What does the research tell us?

Robert C. Solomon and Fernando Flores argue that trust is not something that simply exists naturally – it isn't something we can assume or take for granted. Additionally, it is not a stable or constant quality or "social glue". In our experience, trust can fluctuate even in the course of a single meeting; when people are challenged emotionally, one response is to withdraw trust. Trust in schools is not static – it moves on a continuum. Instead, they believe that trust is an emotional practice – it can be "wilful", voluntary, and a matter of personal responsibility. Flores and Solomon believe that "thinking and talking about trust will not only influence our beliefs but also change our behaviour in the world and with one another". We believe that when leaders truly understand trust and what it looks and sounds like in their settings, they can check themselves and see moments when trust is strong and when trust is being challenged.

In addition to Solomon and Flores' suggestion that trust is a choice – a commitment that leaders should *choose* despite knowing it may lead to betrayal – Stephen Covey in *The Speed of Trust* highlights 13 actions that build trust – when used alongside good words: (1) talk straight, (2) demonstrate respect, (3) create transparency, (4) right wrongs, (5) show loyalty, (6) deliver results, (7) get better, (8) confront reality, (9) clarify expectations, (10) practise accountability, (11) listen first, (12) keep commitments, and (13) extend trust.

Daniel Coyle in *The Culture Code* goes one step further than "listening first" – suggesting we should overcommunicate our listening. In *Fierce Conversations*, Susan Scott recommends we "speak *and listen* as if this is the most important conversation you will ever have…participate as if it matters. It does". There are clear signals leaders can develop to ensure the person they are working with feels seen and heard. These habits will help create safety so that the person they are talking with feels safe to be honest and open. In our experience, leaders who do this well will establish trusting relationships where colleagues will talk about the ground truths, which enables the organisation to improve – and there are often things leaders cannot see by themselves: they are essential to talk about. When leaders have not established these trusting relationships with colleagues, a culture of control and fear can exist, which is often a barrier to improvement – both at an organisational and personal level.

In *Dare to Lead* Brene Brown identifies that a factor that diminishes trust is a lack of connection and empathy. We have worked with leaders in the past who have consistently demonstrated compassion and deep care for those they lead – and this has not been at the detriment to running a high-performing organisation. Daniel Coyle in *The Culture Code* also identifies a warm sense of connection and belonging as being a characteristic of successful groups. Coyle, in *The Culture Playbook*, also suggests high-performing teams have a dual focus: part focus goes to the projects and action in hand; and part focus is on the team's inner-workings. Creating moments to reflect together and learn together generates cohesion and safety – the group can trust that they are in a team that values progress over perfection.

In "The Neuroscience of Trust", Paul Zak reveals that, compared with people at low-trust companies, people at high-trust companies report: 74% less stress, 106% more energy at work, 50% higher productivity, 13% fewer sick days, 76% more engagement, 29% more satisfaction with their lives, and 40% less burn-out. We understand that neuroscience research tells us that trust promotes effective communication and collaboration within teams and, as stated above, can significantly impact employee engagement and overall performance. Trust feels great as it releases the hormone oxytocin and the neurotransmitter dopamine. We have worked with – and led – teams that have been united by a shared vision and are characterised by high levels of trust, groups of people who are equally invested in – and who can all, regardless of their job title, contribute to – the success of the organisation. These are teams full of drive, healthy conflict, care – and, without fail, trust (which fluctuates and moves but remains).

Lastly, in her book *Radical Candour*, Kim Scott defines being radically candid as caring personally while challenging directly. At its core, radical candour is guidance and feedback that's both kind and clear, specific and sincere. Choosing radical candour can help maintain trust in your relationships with colleagues. Brene Brown supports this idea stating "clear is kind". We understand, from our experience, that leaders must value having potentially uncomfortable conversations over their own comfort. To deny colleagues or the organisation these conversations, which promote growth and improvement, undermines trust and is detrimental for future success.

In our experience it is wise to establish agreed ways of working for meetings that are held. We call these above and below the line behaviours. Above the line behaviours are the positive behaviours we would expect to witness with our staff that lead to successful outcomes, e.g. encouraging healthy conflict. Below the line behaviours are those that are detrimental to the performance of the team, e.g. interrupting a colleague because you disagree with their viewpoint.

KEY TAKEAWAYS

- Trust is an emotional practice – it is voluntary and a matter of personal responsibility – and with it comes the possibility of betrayal. Before anything else, leaders must consciously develop this emotional practice – considering the very real cost of betrayal.
- Studies have suggested that employees perform better in high-trust organisations – not only that, but they have more energy, suffer less from stress, and are happier.
- Leaders can deliberately interact with others in a way that increases trust.

After 11 years in education, working in a variety of roles – both pastoral and data – Elliot sits in his car in a near empty car park preparing himself to step through the doors into his new role: his second headship. Elliot glances at his phone as a text comes through from an ex-colleague and mentor; she had messaged him a few lines from the reference she had provided for this new role. This small act generated a sense of pride and belief that he could do the job – and he needed to feel that having read an article online a few days ago suggesting most second headships failed. As Elliot walked through the doors as headteacher, the responsibility to deliver on the vision he'd shared with staff during his appointment felt daunting; Elliot desperately wanted his new staff team to trust that he'd deliver results. Elliot understood that this school is vulnerable; historically, outcomes have been significantly below average and the governors expected change and the school was in an inspection window. Elliot hoped he knew enough – whilst guarding against simply transferring what worked in his first headship to this new setting.

As he entered the school, the caretaker, David, said hello. Elliot understood that every connection he was about to make was important – it would help develop trust. He knew it took a team to create change and everyone was needed. He walked past the canteen on the way to his office; again he was welcomed warmly and he took just a few minutes to recognise each staff member. Elliot made his way upstairs to his first-floor office; the door had been unlocked by the caretaker – no need to fumble with which key he needed. He entered the office, and put down his box of pictures of his family and educational achievements – he could sort them later. Elliot looked out of the window across the school grounds and thought about the upcoming morning senior leadership team meeting. He had met all five of them over the summer break to start building trust, so the relationship had begun – and everyone on the senior leadership team understood their portfolio areas and what was expected of them. Elliot had spent some time over the summer working on the School Improvement Plan – but now he wondered if, at this moment in time, he was best placed to decide what the school needed. At the same time, he felt like he needed an answer for everything. Elliot has been thinking about trust, knowing that for an organisation to be happy and healthy, authentic trust must be built and maintained. From his experience, Elliot felt like trust existed when genuine care and warmth and empathy were embedded in a school community. He remembered the text message he received less than ten minutes ago and smiled.

As he fired up his laptop there was a knock on the door.

Amara stands at the threshold of Elliot's door feeling both apprehensive and excited (Figure 1.1) – she'd not met Elliot other than at the headteacher interview process. she started at her current school as a teacher of English – and is now, very proudly, Head of English. Amara has worked really hard to build positive relationships with her colleagues – some of which she now calls her friends. This could create a challenge for Amara. She knows she has to adapt her relationships with her team and that they will need her to be radically candid in order for the department to improve. Amara still values positive relationships with her team – and wants to nurture these. It is a difficult balance but she is starting the position with trust in the team, and she needs to ensure this trust does not diminish on her drive to improvement.

Amara welcomes Elliot to the school – keen to make a connection. Amara shares her excitement with Elliot about the opportunity to learn and grow together – she knows this is going to be a big year and that the spotlight is firmly on English. On her way down to her new office, Amara feels hopeful that Elliot will create the change that the school and the community desire. At his headteacher presentation he talked about a vision for the school which Amara liked; this vision helped Amara begin to build trust in him – she wanted the same vision for the children and staff at the school.

Marco walks into school fearing opening his emails. He always wants to be positive, and believes as deputy head of a large primary school that's part of his role, even if inside he is worrying. The school has had three headteachers in four years and that's left an impact on the school and its community. He walks towards his office and says a cheery good morning to the staff he meets along the way. He opens his email to the usual barrage of complaints from parents regarding behaviour at the school, children being bullied, pocket money being stolen, and children unable to learn in the classrooms. The school is in an area of poverty; Marco has plenty of friends that work in leafy suburbs who explain how different it is for them, but he loves the school and its community and wants to stay. Deep down he knows what needs to be done, but everytime he begins a new head steps-in and sets their own pathway. The staff have lost trust that the school will ever be led "properly" and every year will see a new vision from a new person at the top that they will never see out. Marco understands it's increasingly difficult to appoint heads in challenging schools; he has personally witnessed some heads suddenly "disappear" during the academic year.

It's been personally difficult for Marco; he invests in relationships with his headteachers only to find they leave. This is emotionally tiring for him. This September sees a new headteacher start again, but after the summer break Marco is keen to go again – the children and staff deserve it and emotionally he needs to build trust with his new leader.

With this in mind, what purposeful steps can Elliot, Amara, and Marco take – and other leaders in similar positions – to build and sustain trust?

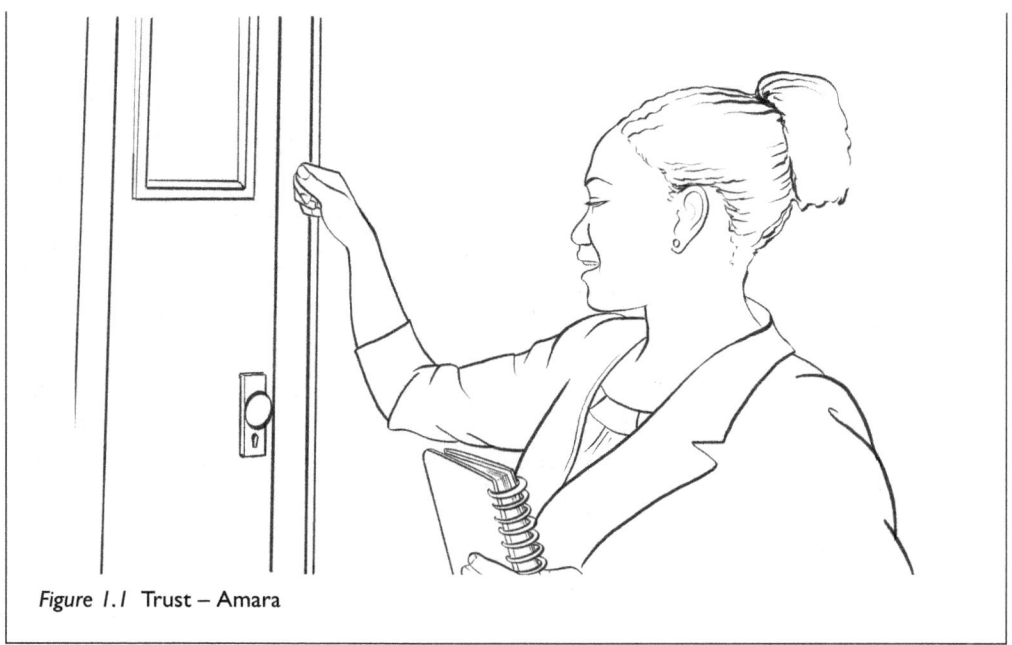

Figure 1.1 Trust – Amara

1. **Think about trust**: before purposeful and deliberate action can be taken to build trust, it is important to attend to your own existing beliefs and practices. The decision to trust is heavily influenced by your own previous experiences of being trusted and moments of betrayal. Solomon and Flores state that "trust is something we do, something we make".

    a. Betrayal: trust brings with it the possibility of betrayal. Building trust means coming to terms with the possibility of breach and betrayal. Consider trust as fragile – it always involves a risk. But understand that "breaches of trust do not mark the end of trust but are part of the process of trusting" (Solomon & Flores). Consider what a breach or betrayal looks like – emotionally safeguard against this.

    b. Judgement: trust is an emotional skill – one that requires judgement, vigilant attention, and deliberate action. The first action is the decision to trust. In your context, should you decide to trust? Because trust is something we do – it isn't something we have. Trust is not earned; it must be given. Most people respond to trust by being trustworthy. Flores and Solomon believe that "the psychological reward of trust is that it is gratifying to be trusted". Consider how you might begin trust with trust.

    c. Freedom: distrust creates restrictions on who you work with – and how you work. Consider what restrictions are in place in your context that are a symptom of distrust?

d. Self-trust: distrust can often be a projection of missing self-trust. Self-trust is about practising kindness and not perfection. It is a refusal to give up on yourself. How strong are your self-trust practices?

   e. Talk and think about trust: thinking and talking about trust will influence our beliefs and change our behaviour in our own context and with the people in it. Talk to your team about trust in your organisation – make it a comfortable conversation: where are there pockets of trust? Where are there pockets of distrust? Where has there been betrayal? What has been done about it?

2. **Make trust visible**: Flores and Solomon suggest that trust often only becomes visible when it has been challenged or violated. Think about what trust looks and feels like in your organisation before it is betrayed. Think about the often subconscious habits and practices that build and maintain trust.

   a. Establish above and below the line behaviours which will allow trust to grow – deliver with absolute clarity – naming the behaviours you'd expect to see (above the line) as well as those you don't want to see (below the line); this empowers the group to challenge actions that erode trust. Look out for: eye rolling, crossing arms, deliberate disengagement, sharpness in tone, and disregarding team's suggestions and ideas without due consideration.

   b. When you spot a below the line behaviour which erodes trust in a team meeting, be prepared to challenge it and hold your team to account – know that it is important enough to feel a moment's discomfort.

   Use the following:

   – *we globally agreed that that is a behaviour we didn't believe is healthy.*

   – *that is a below the line behaviour we all agreed to challenge in this team.*

   c. When you spot someone else on the team challenging a below the line behaviour which can erode trust, recognise it so that it is repeated.

   Use the following:

   – *thank you for challenging that behaviour – you're helping us uphold and develop trust in our team, which is really important to me.*

   – *thank you for recognising that unhelpful behaviour – it's important that we all challenge this and that this is a responsibility shared across the team and doesn't rest solely with me.*

   d. When you identify a behaviour which erodes trust outside of a team meeting, challenge it – but consider when would be best to do so. Your team should protect and uphold trust at all times – if you notice moments where this isn't the case, identify it and challenge it.

Use the following:

- *I noticed that you choose to do X, can you tell me why?*
- *It's important that we fully support each other; I noticed you did X, why did this happen?*

e. You can build trust by ensuring every voice is heard. Take deliberate steps to ensure every member of the team contributes and is able and willing to share their thinking. When everyone has a voice trust is visible. More on this in **Finding Your Voice**.

Use the following:

- *What are you seeing from your perspective?*
- *Your view is different to mine – can you explain your thoughts?*
- *How would you describe what is happening now?*
- *What is your current thinking about X?*

3. **Trust vs control**: does the culture in your school allow staff to complete tasks to move the organisation forwards without the fear of blame or punishment for decisions? How do you ensure that you don't become a "door handle" leader with staff feeling that every decision has to go to your door and come from you?

   a. Ensure that staff portfolio areas have complete clarity, especially senior leaders. Give them the opportunity to genuinely lead on projects and support them as necessary.

   b. When success occurs ensure that you recognise the staff involved, and put them ahead of your own ego. Look out of the window when you have success but look in the mirror when challenges occur.

   c. It's easy to lose trust, and this can occur during times when you are under the most pressure. At times when you have to prepare a governor report, emails to respond to, staff that need to talk with you, and a parent in reception with a complaint, remember: when you walk the corridor remain polite, professional, and approachable. There is nothing wrong with explaining that you can't have the conversation with a staff member there and then, but they are important in the organisation's success – don't lose their trust by disregarding or ignoring them.

   d. If the above occurs, have the humility to speak with the staff member to apologise. Just because it has a title on your door doesn't make you beyond an apology. Staff understand that you are under pressure and that occasionally our own emotional intelligence is challenged.

e. Can you leave your organisation or department for a day without your mobile phone repeatedly going off for decisions to be made? If not, reflect on why this is happening. We understand that headteachers have to make certain decisions around exclusions/suspensions but why are you needed to make all the others? The sign of a good leader is one that can leave for a day (or even for a new role away from your current school) and the organisation still flourishes.

4. Purposefully build trusting relationships

a. Taking a genuine interest in the people you work with – their lives, their challenges, their families, their aspirations – is one of the strongest ways to build trusting relationships. The people you work with should feel safe to share what they're thinking and feeling – and that this will be validated and listened to.

b. Coyle (2019) suggests leaders should preview future connections – it can connect "the dots between where the players were and where they were headed".

> "In three years time, we will be..."
>
> "I think we'll look back to this moment and think..."
>
> "This time next year we will be..."

c. Talk about your expectations – talk about how high and how ambitious your expectations are, knowing that positive expectations influence performance positively (The Pygmalion Effect):

> "I have the highest expectations of you. And I know you can meet them".

d. Coyle (2019) highlights the importance of overdoing thank yous – because "it has less to do with thanks than affirming the relationship". Offering frequent, genuine, and specific thank yous creates belonging and connectedness and can generate cooperative behaviours. Share your thank yous face to face, and by email – rereading a thank you email after a tough day can be hugely uplifting.

e. James Kerr (2013) shares the concept of sweeping the sheds – the idea that everyone is responsible for the smallest details; you are never too big to do the small jobs. When leaders sweep the sheds, the staff team can strive collectively towards achieving the team's highest potential. Coyle (2019) calls this "muscular humility – a mindset of seeking simple ways to serve the group". This could be displayed by a leader picking up rubbish or helping to put the chairs away at the end of a meeting.

5. **Overcommunicate your listening**: build trust with the people you work with by overcommunicating your listening; ensure that colleagues feel seen and heard – that their part in your organisation is important and valued.

   a. Remove all distractions to ensure you can listen to understand: put phones away, close emails, put a sign on the door. And explain this to the person you're talking to:

      – *I'm closing my door/emails because I want to listen to you.*

      Alternatively, if the time isn't right, then rearrange the meeting:

      – *I want to really listen so can we meet later today?*

   b. Body language: people within successful cultures use body language to signal trust and safety:

      – Be still.

      – Lean towards the speaker.

      – Maintain soft eye contact.

      – The only sound should be a steady stream of affirmations (*yes, uh-huh*).

   c. Embrace silence: listen first, speak last.

      Use moments of silence to purposefully slow down the conversation so that you can begin to discover the problem – not just the symptom. When you jump to fill the silence with your own voice, you're not learning anything you didn't already know.

   d. Seek to understand: everyone owns a different version of reality – encourage open and honest conversation by uncovering their reality:

      – *keep talking*

      – *say more about that*

      – *tell me more*

      – *what else?*

      – *talk to me about...*

   e. Ask for more: to ensure conversations are rich and useful – and that you overcommunicate your listening – use the following questions:

      – *what is the most important thing we've discussed so far today?*

- *how is this currently impacting you?*

- *what else?*

- *what are some of the possible actions?*

- *what is your next step following our conversations?*

- *how are you feeling about this conversation?*

References

Brown, B. (2019) *Dare to Lead*. Random House Publishing.
Covey, S. (2008) *The Speed of Trust*. Simon & Schuster.
Coyle, D. (2019) *The Culture Code*. Random House Publishing.
Coyle, D. (2022) *The Culture Playbook*. Cornerstone Press.
Kerr, J. (2013) *Legacy. What the All Blacks Can Teach Us about the Business of Life*. Constable.
Scott, K. (2019) *Radical Candour*. Pan.
Scott, S. (2017) *Fierce Conversations*. Piaktus.
Solomon, R. C. and Flores, F. (2003) *Building Trust: In Business, Politics, Relationships, and Life*. Oxford University Press.
Zak, P. (2017) The neuroscience of trust. *Harvard Business Review*, 95(1), 84–90.

2 Vulnerability

What does the research tell us?

Brene Brown in *Dare to Lead* (2019) clearly positions vulnerability as a strength and, in fact, a necessary leadership behaviour in order to create braver leaders and courageous cultures – which is what our schools need and deserve. Brown explains that "courage and fear are not mutually exclusive. Most of us feel brave and afraid at the exact same time. We feel vulnerable". School leaders might feel vulnerable on their way to a meeting, or when delivering to staff or visitors, or perhaps they feel it all day long. Brown believes that "our ability to be daring leaders will never be greater than our capacity for vulnerability". In order to lean into vulnerability, Brown suggests we must "cultivate a culture in which brave work, tough conversations, and whole hearts are the expectation, and armour is not necessary or rewarded". In our experience, some of the strongest leaders we've had the privilege of working with in the schools that we have led have been those willing to engage fully in tough conversations – both delivering them and receiving them. We wonder whether new leaders find vulnerability more challenging and that possibly experience and success make vulnerability easier. However, leading through the really tough times, when you feel like you're failing and success feels elusive and unattainable, is *exactly* when school leaders need to demonstrate genuine vulnerability and to welcome healthy conflict and tough conversations. Daniel Coyle in *The Culture Code* (2019) believes this culture can be created when the leader is vulnerable first and often, and that "group cooperation is created by small, frequently repeated moments of vulnerability" adding that "none carries more power than the moment when a leader signals vulnerability". In our experience of leading schools, we believe that the conversations and moments to establish vulnerability happen frequently and are often in our day-to-day conversations with all staff, and are not limited to, but can be further established, in formal meetings. Coyle goes on to explore that "at some level, we intuitively know that vulnerability tends to spark cooperation and trust". Interestingly, Coyle's examination of Dr Jeff Polzer's work (a professor of organisational behaviour at Harvard) reveals that vulnerability is "less about the sender than the receiver". This interaction is called the vulnerability loop: "a shared exchange of openness, it's the most basic building block of cooperation and trust", which appears to be contagious; "the feelings of trust and closeness sparked by the vulnerability loop were transferred in full strength to someone who simply happened to be in the room". Additionally, In *Legacy*, James Kerr (2013) states "the key to trusting peer-to-peer interactions is a high level of trust. This is trust in the sense of safe vulnerability". We believe that, when time pressured, and in stressful situations, school leaders need to be mindful of maintaining trusting peer-to-peer interactions; school leaders need to manage those short, unexpected, corridor conversations with great care and should act to purposefully maintain trust and vulnerability. We consider these moments in schools to be the times when you are at most risk of damaging previous healthy relationships.

Brown believes that "if we're brave enough often enough, we will fall". If we shield ourselves from uncertainty, risk, emotional exposure, tough feedback, and vulnerability, we will stop growing as leaders. But it takes courage to turn up when you can't control the outcome. School leaders have the courage to turn up when they don't have all the answers. We believe, from our experience, that effective school leaders ensure they have created an environment rooted in trust and vulnerability, which empowers all to have their voice heard and contribute to the direction of the organisation. Brown suggests leaders must "choose courage over comfort". Coyle proposes that "exchanges of vulnerability, which we naturally tend to avoid, are the pathway through which trusting cooperation is built". Disrupters and agitators – crucial for healthy conflict and growth in any team – must deliver the message consistently and repeatedly: *it is safe to tell the truth here, even if it is uncomfortable.*

Brown identifies unhelpful leadership behaviours which are unclear and unkind:

> not getting clear with a colleague about your expectations because it feels too hard yet holding them accountable or blaming them for not delivering is unkind. Talking about people rather than to them is unkind. Feeding people half-truths to make them feel better (which is almost always about making ourselves feel more comfortable) is unkind.

Daring leadership is ultimately about serving other people – which is why we choose to be clear knowing that "clear is kind".

Brown explores that in "tough conversations, hard meetings, and emotionally charged decision making, leaders need the grounded confidence to stay tethered to their values, respond rather than react emotionally, and operate from self-awareness, not self-protection". Who you are is how you lead. Susan Scott in *Fierce Leadership* (2011) believes that leaders, and the people we lead, fear "the consequences of authenticity – intimacy and vulnerability. We fear being real, being ourselves, disclosing our real thoughts and feelings, being seen, being known. It's time to change all that". Scott highlights just how important it is to change as "when life is primarily about creating safety, we are in no danger of becoming the change agents who bring our highest and best to our own lives much less to those around us". Scott thinks leaning into vulnerability means you can stop playing not to lose, and start playing to win. In our experience of leading schools, organisations that are not trusting and are not safe enough to be vulnerable are where a fear of failure can inhibit improvement. Organisations which are playing to win are places where trust and vulnerability give school leaders silent permission to make bold and brave decisions that are different and potentially risky – particularly when our external accountability measures are at play. Similarly, Patrick Lencioni in *The Advantage* (2012) affirms that "at the heart of vulnerability lies the willingness of people to abandon their pride and their fear, to sacrifice their egos for the collective good of the team". The importance of vulnerability in leadership is strengthened by Rob Coe in the 2022 Great Teaching Toolkit "School Environment and Leadership: Evidence Review" which highlights the need for leaders to be willing "to share or expose vulnerabilities" as well as establish and maintain "feelings of psychological safety: it is ok to take a risk or make a mistake".

Interestingly, Jacob Morgan in *Leading with Vulnerability* (2024) states that "vulnerability is not always a good thing at work, especially if you are not highly competent at your job" and that it cannot be used as a "crutch to justify ongoing poor performance". Morgan creates a clear distinction between being vulnerable and being a vulnerable leader. In our leadership experience of improving schools we believe that, whilst maintaining trust and demonstrating vulnerability, it is still ultimately the leader's job to set the direction and be held accountable for the organisation. Leaders cannot hide behind the type of vulnerability that leads to ineffectiveness and a lack of growth – it must benefit the team (Table 2.1).

Table 2.1 Vulnerability

Vulnerable	**Vulnerable Leader**
Admitting to a mistake	Admitting to a mistake **and sharing what was learned.**
Asking for help	Asking for help **and committing to learning what you need help with.**
Showing emotion	Showing emotion **but practising self-awareness to be conscientious of how that emotion comes across and the impact it can have.**
Saying "I don't know"	Saying "I don't know" **but having an idea or a plan for how to figure it out.**
Talking about personal challenges or struggles	Talking about personal challenges or struggles **for the purpose of connecting, creating trust and relatability, as opposed to a therapy session.**
Being unsure	Being unsure **but having a vision for where you want to end up.**

Source: Morgan (2024).

KEY TAKEAWAYS

- Vulnerability in leadership is the emotion leaders experience during times of uncertainty, risk, and emotional exposure: it is a strength.
- Studies have suggested that in order to create cooperation, vulnerability is a psychological requirement.
- Embracing habits of vulnerability can create discomfort – and these habits need relentless repetition. Leaders must be willing to make themselves vulnerable – first and often – to get the best from the people they lead.
- Ambitious, brave leadership requires vulnerability.
- When it comes to vulnerability, it is important for it not to become self-indulgent; it must benefit the team and help move the organisation forwards.

Elliot feels proud to have made an impact in his first half-term. He knew it would be challenging to establish himself and start to provide a clear direction for the school. Elliot ensures that he knows all the staff names and uses them to greet each one. He is also proud of learning more and more of the student names as the term progressed.

However, Elliot has a concern. In the staff and senior leadership meetings he feels like it has been his voice alone setting the direction and Elliot planning his values and vision for the school. He knows that he has to develop other staff so that they contribute to decisions that are for the good of the school. Elliot knows that he doesn't have all the answers and that the collective intelligence of the group will make success much more attainable. He is certain that he has the right leaders at the school but they appear used to simply being instructed what to do or simply agree with the previous head's ideas. Elliot needs to shift this thinking to benefit the children and the organisation. Elliot knows that he has established healthy meeting behaviours within the senior leadership team and that these are helping to build and maintain trust. Elliot wonders whether the next step is to make sure it is safe enough for all staff to be vulnerable – he knows that leading with vulnerability is one of the most powerful things he can do to create stronger connections, continue to build trust, and to unlock the potential of the staff around him.

Amara is pleased with her contribution to the English team, and has built a strong relationship with the headteacher in a short period of time; she has felt that her Line Management meetings have been prioritised and consistent – on the occasion Elliot was called into an emergency meeting, he rearranged the meeting for the next day. Amara ensures that she is accountable for the tasks given to her and she never misses an action point for the following week's meeting. Often Amara will take ideas from her Line Management meeting and action them with the English Team, ensuring that the staff in her department complete each task with diligence. Before each Line Management meeting she checks that her staff have updated the electronic forms to capture the information required. Despite feeling positive about the direction the team are going in, Amara feels that they are lacking in initiative and often feel like she's the only one pushing for better. In addition to this, Amara has presented a professional front with the team, and she is really missing the connection she had with them prior to taking on the role as Head of English.

Marco has decided that this term is the time to improve areas within his portfolio area; he is tired at the continual shift of direction from the past frequent change of leadership regarding behaviour at the school – the school deserved better, and so did Marco. The new head has explained to Marco that he has autonomy to develop his own pathway with how to improve behaviour at the school. Marco feels nervous and excited, and he doesn't have all the answers and that makes him slightly worried; he questions: how will he succeed? How can he do it on his own without direct instruction from his headteacher? Marco has never had such freedom to lead, but with this freedom comes accountability. The new headteacher has shown trust in Marco and he is starting to trust her.

Marco believes that a positive behaviour for learning approach would be a great initiative for the school – he has watched this work in schools he has visited but he also knows it needs adapting to fit his school community. Marco knows that some of the staff at school want poorly behaved children to be removed from the school, and others want to keep them in class as they are often the children from poverty. Marco knows he needs to establish a clear direction. He now knows his first step: speak with the senior leadership team and the staff body to explain that, at the moment, he doesn't have all the answers but it's his intention to use the collective intelligence at the school – and other schools – to make the school community one the whole staff body can be proud off (and remove some of the daily fear of opening emails) (Figure 2.1).

Figure 2.1 Vulnerability – Marco

> With this in mind, what purposeful steps can Elliot, Amara, and Marco take – and other leaders in similar positions – to embrace and encourage vulnerability?

1. **Create a designed space to show vulnerability**: senior leaders can create the opportunity to demonstrate vulnerability, drive the organisation forwards, and use collective intelligence via the use of a process called Sightlines (see appendix for a template example). This can be used both at department and senior leader level (and others). Sightlines are a timed activity and must be well led for maximum impact:

    a. Identify your problem of practice from your portfolio area. Explain to the team your issues and what you wish to improve. Headteachers should also present their own problem of practice (they don't have all the answers!).

    b. The team should ask clarifying questions around the problem of practice; this allows all leaders to have their own thinking checked for understanding and allows vulnerability.

    c. The member of staff presenting then answers all the clarifying questions asked and provides further information as required.

    d. Then the whole group feedback their thinking and advice around the problem of practice. The presenter must listen to this advice in silence (see steps in the appendix) and allow all the group to have their input. For some leaders this can be a challenge; they are often used to thinking they must have all the answers or must jump in and interrupt others' thinking!

    e. The presenter must then explain what actions they are going to take and then report back to the group when they close their sightline (this also has a process attached). All group members are accountable to the group, and we use the power of the group to change the group in terms of vulnerability, timelines, shared thinking, accountability, and moving the organisation forwards.

2. **Create a psychologically safe environment**: everyone feels safe to be vulnerable and talk about what has gone wrong – as well as celebrating what has gone well.

    a. Spotlight your own fallibility in order to encourage others to talk about their own moments of failure – the opposite would mean your colleagues aim to hide mistakes.

    > "Can anyone spot where I've gone wrong?"

    > "Can you see if I've made mistakes with this?"

"I couldn't get X to work – can you see how it might?"

"I just couldn't find the solution to X, can you?"

"I'd planned to do X, but I got Y. Are you able to tell me where I went wrong?"

b. Ask for help – make it an acceptable habit to tap into the power of the team:

"I need your help with X, do you think you can help me?"

"I'm certain the answer is in the room – can you share your thoughts?"

"This is the first attempt/draft at X – I need your help to make it better: what can you do?"

"Can you tell me what we're missing here?"

c. Make yourself vulnerable first by welcoming feedback on your leadership habits by actively asking for it:

"What can I do to make you more effective?"

"What's one skill/talent/experience you have that I've overlooked/undervalued?"

"What is one thing I do that helps the team to be successful?"

"What is one thing I don't currently do/don't do frequently enough that you think I should do more often?"

d. Undertake a pre-mortem with your team – this will begin to create safety around talking about failure and bad news before it has actually happened. As Coyle explains, "this kind of signal is not just an admission of weakness; it's also an invitation to create deeper connection, because it sparks a response in the listener: *How can I help?*".

"What could go wrong with this?"

"What might be some problems we encounter with this?"

"Why might we fail with this?"

"How will we know if this is working or failing?"

"What early signs should we look out for that might suggest X isn't going well?"

(Find out more about how to run an effective pre-mortem in Section 2, Chapter 13: Making Decisions)

e. Talk about your areas for development – and what you're doing to get better. It isn't enough to talk about your weaknesses – as Morgan states, vulnerability can never be a crutch for ongoing poor performance:

"I really struggle with X, so I've recently been reading about…and have learnt…"

"I've been struggling with X, so I have done Y".

"I'd really like your feedback on X because it is an area I'm working on at the moment".

"I think I could improve X, so I'd like you to spot when I do Y and let me know so that I can get better".

3. **How to manage healthy conflict**: leaders must engineer "intelligent, spirited conversation" (Scott, 2011) by creating and celebrating healthy conflict. Set a tone that makes healthy conflict not only encouraged – but also expected.

   a. Let your team know that you *want* conflict – and explain why. Repeat this message frequently – in staff meetings, in department meetings, etc.:

   "Healthy conflict is important and expected in this team".

   "Conflict might feel uncomfortable – but it is necessary".

   "Without conflict, we lose our greatest opportunity for improvement".

   "Conflict gets us to a better place".

   "Conflict is part of what makes us a great team".

   "We will disagree – we will experience conflict – it is always for the good of the team/organisation".

   b. Model how to receive conflict – ask for disagreement and critique, and then create the team norms when receiving it:

   "Thank you for sharing that; I know it'll help me improve".

   "Thank you for sharing your perspective – it is important that I hear from you all".

   "It is great that you are disagreeing with me – it's a sign of a great team".

   c. Crome (2023) suggests leaders should introduce conflict deliberately by starting with a topic that will generate different opinions:

   "I'd like us to talk about X because I'm hoping there will be different opinions and we can all engage in some healthy conflict".

"I think this topic will help us practise how to respond to challenge – knowing it is always for the team and never personal".

"I'm hoping we can create some healthy conflict and challenge today by discussing X".

d. Spotlight and celebrate conflict and challenge when it happens. Lencioni (2012) believes this is the time leaders should interrupt, which can feel counterintuitive but gives people permission to engage fully and lets them know that what they are doing is desirable – it makes a team stronger:

"What is happening now is great – this challenge will help us unlock greatness".

"X and Y, this conflict you're about to engage in is exactly what we need. Please continue".

"X, you are providing us with a perfect model of how to receive challenge – with respect and curiosity".

"This is what we look like when we're at our best! Keep going!"

e. Respond swiftly to a lack of engagement in conflict – or reactions which shut-down conflict and challenge in the team. Clear is kind:

"It feels like you're holding back your opinion at times, can you tell me about that?"

"I noticed that when X challenged you in our meeting you responded by doing Y. Talk to me about that".

"I need the team to engage in conflict and challenge – how do you feel about that?"

"Your response to X's challenge shut-down further conflict, which is unhealthy for the group. Talk to me about what you were thinking".

4. **Embracing failure**: sharing and embracing failure with your team help yourself and others to learn, and change the narrative around failure. We believe that great leaders will all experience failure at times, and this is often linked to future success. Success and failure are partners and are not enemies.

   a. When you fail, because you will, you need to be kind and curious. Clarity on what went wrong is important, but this should not be debilitating. You should guard against being consumed by moments of failure – it's a moment in time. Take time to look at what went wrong, what *parts* failed – create distance and remove your personality from it – think of the actions that did not create the outcome you intended.

b. At times failure will hurt, which can be inevitable. It's fine to feel hurt and upset that the planning hasn't provided the outcomes you desired. But don't allow that to stop you from learning from failure – to remove this would inhibit your development and that of the school.

c. Share your failure with your team and allow your team to break the issues down for you; how can you use their feedback to feed into future success? This use of collective intelligence will be invaluable to you and the organisation. Great leaders will move towards failures and not hide them away. We aim to become experts in all that we do and our failures will identify the areas we might be novices at.

d. As a leader, staff will want to see how you respond to other people's failure. Do you lay blame at their door or do you support them by embracing failure and learning all we can from it. Leaders should respond to other colleagues' failure with kindness, as that is what we would desire.

e. Where possible leaders should use failures to plan for future success. If fully embraced, failure can provide the pathway to success. However, leaders should have the confidence to say 'I don't know'. It is then a leader's responsibility to identify solutions to problems of practice.

5. **Vulnerable leadership isn't about oversharing** – it is not about always talking openly about your struggles and your emotions. Great leaders aren't afraid to be vulnerable – but a vulnerable leader can be one that discloses very little about their personal life.

    a. Choose vulnerability that improves the team and the organisation – demonstrate vulnerability around failure and curiosity and continuous professional growth.

    b. Tell your team when things are feeling hard; you shouldn't arrive at work with armour on. You can model this for your team, by telling them: "I'm really struggling at the moment" without feeling the need to disclose all your personal details.

    c. Tell your team what support looks like – what would help you during this time? Your colleagues will want to support you – even if it is just with a cup of tea.

    d. Consider your boundaries: boundaries and professional standards reign at work. Your school is not always the right place to speak openly about your personal life – you are in a professional setting.

    e. Ensure that you have people around you – family and/or friends – that you can talk to without holding back – these are the right people to share the emotional labour with.

References

Brown, B. (2019) *Dare to Lead*. Random House Publishing.

Coe, R., Kime, S. and Singleton, D. (2022). *A Model for School Environment and Leadership (School Environment and Leadership: Evidence Review)*. Evidence Based Education.

Coyle, D. (2019) *The Culture Code*. Random House Publishing.

Crome, S. (2023) *The Power of Teams: How to Create and Lead Thriving School Teams*. John Catt.

Kerr, J. (2013) *Legacy. What the All Blacks Can Teach Us about the Business of Life*. Constable.

Lencioni, P. (2012) *The Advantage. Why Organisational Health Trumps Everything Else in Business*. Jossey-Bass.

Morgan, J. (2024) *Leading with Vulnerability* Jon Wiley & Sons, Inc.

Scott, S. (2011) *Fierce Leadership: A Bold Alternative to the Worst 'Best Practices' of Business Today*. Piatkus.

3 Vision

What does the research tell us?

Patrick Lencioni in *The Advantage* (2012) offers the following definition of a leadership team: "a small group of people who are collectively responsible for achieving a common objective for their organisation". In order for a team to actively work towards achieving a common objective, they need a vision for the future. This vision for a school, or group of schools, is best created by engaging with all the key stakeholders both within, and external to, the organisation. In our experience a lack of vision, or the clarity of it, can be debilitating for the employees. We believe everyone needs a "why" to be most effective. In "Creating a Vision for Your Change" the NHS suggests that an attractive picture of the future "provides a foundation for planning our actions, helping us to understand the gap between the present and the desired future state". Identifying this gap is crucial to any effective school improvement planning.

Lencioni (2012) also considers the impact of a leadership without a common vision and alignment: "just a little daylight between members of a leadership team becomes blinding and overwhelming to employees one or two levels below" stating that "leaders underestimate the impact of even subtle misalignment at the top, and the damage caused to the rest of the organisation". It is clear that directional alignment and a common vision of the future are necessary. Alongside values, its vision should guide every aspect of a school – from strategy and school improvement planning to hiring staff. Leaders should consider how intolerant they are of tasks, actions, and language that undermine the vision for their organisation. We believe that school leaders need to be prepared to protect the vision and call out anything that undermines or challenges this. When done well – with trust, vulnerability, and real clarity – the vision becomes important to the whole organisation and every member of the current and future staff team protects it – values and vision become, powerfully, how things are done.

Simon Sinek in *Start with Why* believes great leadership requires two things: "a vision of the world that does not yet exist and the ability to communicate it".

Further to this, in his book *Leaders Eat Last*, Sinek explains that when a leader creates a captivating vision worthy of time and energy, the release of dopamine creates feelings of excitement and compels us to engage and commit to taking steps towards the vision; dopamine helps us "work tirelessly to realise an imagined vision of the future". Interestingly, Sinek explores the idea that:

> the best visions offer us something that, for all practical purposes, we will never actually reach, but for which we'd gladly die trying. Each point in our journey is an opportunity to feel like we're making progress toward something bigger than ourselves.

From our experience of leading school teams, regular recognition of movement of the organisation towards the vision should be shared and celebrated with all – this is compelling and motivating for all staff. Success stories are chosen wisely and shared widely. These regular moments of reflection and recognition also provide leaders with an opportunity to shift and adjust where necessary. The vision doesn't change – but the steps to get there might.

Mark Cole believes that "without vision, a leader cannot lead". Cole explores John Maxwell's final leadership quality from his book *The 21 Indispensable Qualities of a Leader – Becoming a Person Others Will Want to Follow*, which is vision. Cole helpfully makes three summaries: (1) vision comes from within, (2) vision comes from your history, and (3) vision should meet the needs of another. We believe that Cole's three summaries create a challenge for school leaders – should a school's vision come from one leader, and from their history? Or, with an effective school community around them, should a vision come from all stakeholders?

Communicating a vision is just as critical as creating it. In *Start with Why* Sinek explains that "great leaders and great organisations are good at seeing what most of us can't see. They are good at giving us things we would never think of asking for". Because ambitious and compelling visions aren't within our eyesight, we need leaders to articulate them clearly and concisely and consistently. This means leaders must have absolute clarity about what their vision looks like day to day, and what it doesn't look like, and be willing to challenge this to protect their vision for the future desired state.

Ambition Institute suggests that, without a vision, schools "stand less of a chance of growing, expanding and improving because of the lack of clear direction". When we consider a lack of growth and improvement may equate to student outcomes, the need for a vision and direction becomes a significant concern for school leaders. Ambition Institute suggests five ways to ensure a school's vision becomes meaningfully embedded in everyday life: (1) keep it visible, (2) get everyone on board, (3) value employment engagement, (4) use a variety of channels, and (5) choose your stories wisely. We believe that school leaders will know if their vision is visible when every stakeholder is able to confidently articulate the vision and why it is important for that organisation. In the schools we have led, keeping the vision visible has meant removing superfluous, distracting information and keeping the main thing, the main thing. The vision, when visible, is also part of day-to-day conversations and meetings – decisions are made with the vision as the anchor.

> **KEY TAKEAWAYS**
>
> - Identifying a vision creates clarity and understanding of the gap between the current state and the future desired state.
> - Communicating a compelling vision appeals to our innate desire to contribute to something bigger than ourselves – it is part of human nature.
> - Clarity around vision equips leaders with an understanding of the behaviours which promote, and behaviours which undermine the vision.

Elliot starts his second term at the school and is pleased that all his leadership team are now contributing to the school's success by utilising collective intelligence. He provided clear opportunities for this to happen and is always keen to share success stories when his leadership team created positive change. However, Elliot is also certain that the leadership team, and in all probability the staff teams across the school, have no clear vision for the school – apart from all understanding they have a part to play. But a part to play to achieve what future? Are they all aligned, or is it simply "we must get better"? Elliot understands that vision is important (Figure 3.1). At the start of his first headship Elliot thought vision was just a marketing tool and probably of little real value to a school. However, as his first headship progressed he developed an understanding that vision was very important to success and he had witnessed its power.

Elliot understood that to develop the school to its full potential he has to develop a vision that is attractive to all stakeholders, not just himself. This isn't going to be a vision to achieve the best grade from some external judgement – his staff and the children deserve more than this, and Elliot knows he is not going to achieve buy-in from the canteen or maintenance staff from an arbitrary measure – and these staff matter to both him and the success of the school.

Amara has developed her English department's vision to align with the one for the school. Amara has developed this herself and has put in hours away from the school site to ensure if asked she could explain her vision. The vision she was using was one that had been at the school for several years, even though she had to find it herself on the website and it was never referenced in the meeting that she held or had attended.

Amara was sure that no one within her department, which contained some newly qualified teachers, understood the department's (or school's) vision, or really why it even mattered. Amara also understands that the vision can't simply be her version of what she thinks. She has held developments for her department tightly to herself previously;

she thought this was what it meant to be a leader. Now she often thinks about the "tights" and "loose" of processes and wants all her staff to contribute to the vision; she has to let go and loosen some of the tights so all can achieve buy-in and create a shared preferred future for the department.

Marco has met with his senior leadership team and staff body to explain what he wants to achieve for the families the school serves. He explained that he didn't have all the answers but that he was prepared to give everything to improve the school behaviour. The headteacher thanked him following the staff meeting for being so open and honest – it was clear to her and the staff body how much the school means to him. Staff want him to succeed; he has built trust over the years at the school – he was the one consistent amongst an ever-changing leadership team. Marco could have moved on with his experience but he hasn't; staff understand that this was because he was committed to the school – it wasn't simply a stepping stone for him and, importantly, the school staff believe in him. He now wants to make calm classrooms and corridors the norm at his school. This isn't the norm at the moment and hasn't been for many years. Classroom walks currently demonstrate children shouting at each other and at their teachers – and corridors are characterised by chaos with children pushing and shoving. Previous heads had said it was all fine and that this was typical of primary schools post-Covid. The staff body, however, felt sure it was not typical, and Marco had seen good staff leave the school due to behaviour – those that he had stayed in touch with commenting on how much better it was at their new schools. Marco knows what he wants to achieve; he has witnessed it work in other similar school settings, so now he has a vision and so did staff, but how does that vision become a reality?

Figure 3.1 Vision – Elliot

> With this in mind, what purposeful steps can Elliot, Amara, and Marco take – and other leaders in similar positions – to create a compelling and powerful vision?

1. **Think about vision** – understand why your school or team needs a vision – and what will happen without one. A vision for a school and team allows all stakeholders to centre decisions based on what the ultimate aim is and stops us from deviating from the agreed ultimate purpose. We should dream big with our vision. As the leader, you will want to involve all stakeholders – but you must start the thinking; you can't arrive with nothing.

   a. What is it that you aspire for your organisation? What is the big dream? Write this down so that you have clarity.

   b. How far forwards should you dream? Is your vision for your school or team for 1 year, 3 years, or 15 years? When will your vision be a reality?

   c. Consider how far away you currently are from your vision.

   d. Distil your vision down into a few words, or one short sentence. You might need to do this multiple times before you land on the one that feels right.

   e. Check: are you mistaking vision for mission statement and values?

2. **Involve all stakeholders**: be prepared to lead vision meetings and discussions with all your stakeholders. For your vision to be successful it needs to be owned by everyone. Lencioni (2012) suggests the following guiding questions, which can be used to organise discussions:

   a. Why do we exist? You might like to guide your stakeholders to consider both where your organisation or team have come from – and the long-term destination.

   b. How do we behave? Direct your stakeholders to consider the behaviours and habits necessary to arrive at the desired future state: your vision? How will the values help you arrive at your destination?

   c. What do we do? And how will we succeed? It is useful for your stakeholders to consider: what do we want to be the best at? Because schools and teams within schools do many things. It is important to think strategically – what steps and actions can stakeholders take (community, students, governors, etc.) to move the organisation closer to the vision?

   d. What's most important, right now? Lencioni suggests that "if everything is important, then nothing is". You can inspire and motivate your team by identifying the immediate and short-term actions, which will start your journey.

   e. Who must do what? To create autonomy and agency, ensure all stakeholders know how to feed into the vision.

3. **Ensure you have the tools to achieve the vision**: it is important that the school has the tools to achieve its vision – or at least drive towards it.

   a. How have you allocated your budget to allow your vision to be achieved? The vision will be written proudly throughout your school's development plan so align the necessary resources to each area (whilst recognising schools do not always have the necessary budgets!).

   b. Do you need to consider the staff's time? If you have developed a new vision for the school or your team do you need to allocate additional time to make it live? Might you need to consider removing time from another area? As a leader you cannot simply add layers of work onto your staff if you hope to keep them. Everything that we allocate time to is an opportunity cost of not having that time for something else – what is your priority? As a leader the question is "what time is wasted on activities not aligned with the vision?"

   c. Do you have the creativity within your staff team to make the vision a reality? Creativity and innovation amongst the staff team can drive the school towards its vision in ways that leaders may not have considered. Create spaces where staff can present ideas to leaders, work in groups, and problem-solve.

   d. Empower others with the vision. Leaders that empower their co-workers by giving them the authority to lead on areas of the vision create a staff team that feel invested in its success.

   e. Practise patience as a leadership tool. It will take time to achieve big goals, and be careful that you and your staff do not burn out or become frustrated. Set clear and realistic timelines and expectations. Change is a process not an event.

4. **Behave consistently with the vision**: All leaders and staff need to ensure that they behave consistently with the vision.

   a. Every leader needs to protect the vision if it is to be successful. A vision becomes highly vulnerable if staff witness leaders not aligning with it. If staff hear one thing and see another your vision is over. Protect it.

   b. Leaders should foster a positive attitude towards the shared vision. Leaders who communicate their vision with enthusiasm and energy are much more likely to engage their staff with it. Even on a dark, wet and windy school day be the light for your vision.

   c. Once leaders behave consistently with the vision it is their responsibility to ensure that staff also align with it. Always challenge staff that go against the vision. Be consistent.

d. When appointing new staff ensure that the school's vision is part of the questions asked at the interview. If staff do not feel they can align with this vision is the school right for them?

e. Encourage feedback on the vision. How will you know if leaders and staff are behaving consistently with the vision? Is it just your opinion as a leader that matters? Promote staff and stakeholder feedback to provide a more accurate picture of the ground truths.

5. **Make it visible and celebrate small wins**: once you have your school vision you need to ensure that it's highly visible. There is little point having developed your vision and for it never to live in the organisation.

   a. Repeat your vision at staff and department meetings so that it is reencountered at all opportunities. All members of staff need to understand the vision, not simply the teaching personnel. How will you ensure the cleaners, maintenance, catering, and office staff, and other key members understand and live the vision?

   b. Have the vision displayed where decisions are made. Where are the big decisions made? Ensure you have vision displayed in these rooms – this allows us to recentre on our vision when making the key decisions.

   c. Use corridors as a visual aid to display the vision; this allows both children and staff to see it on a daily basis. Schools can use large graphics/vinyls to create cost-effective displays.

   d. Ensure that at least once a month you celebrate the school's success towards reaching its vision. Think about how many children have benefited that month from your vision and share it across all stakeholders.

   e. Consider how to celebrate staff that have enabled the school to move closer to its vision. A letter home from the headteacher or head of department can be greatly appreciated.

References

ACT Academy, NHS Improvement. "Creating a vision for your change." *NHS England*, https://www.england.nhs.uk/wp-content/uploads/2021/06/01-NHS104-Phase-2-Creating-a-vision-for-your-change-210817-A.pdf. Accessed 7 July 2024.

Cole, M. (2020) *Clear Vision*. Mark Cole: Clear Vision - John Maxwell. https://www.maxwellleadership.com/blog/mark-cole-clear-vision/ Accessed 7 July 2024.

Lencioni, P. (2012) *The Advantage. Why Organisational Health Trumps Everything Else in Business*. Jossey-Bass.

Monteith, A. (2018) *5 Tips on Communicating Your Vision and Values*. How to Communicate Vision and Values | Ambition Institute. https://www.ambition.org.uk/blog/5-tips-communicating-your-vision-and-values/ Accessed 7 July 2024.

Sinek, S. (2011) *Start with Why: How Great Leaders Inspire Everyone to Take Action*. Portfolio / Penguin.

4 Clarity

What does the research tell us?

Lencioni (2012) believes that creating clarity is fundamental to creating a healthy organisation, and he states "creating clarity is all about achieving alignment". In fact, Lencioni suggests that leaders should create so much clarity that "there is little room as possible for confusion, disorder and infighting" and that the responsibility for creating this level of clarity lies solely with the leadership team. Further to this, Lencioni explores the cause of a lack of clarity and alignment in an organisation – and that a leader's natural response is to see it as a "behavioural or attitudinal problem" rather than a failing on their part. In our experience, school leaders should consider which aspects of the organisation would benefit from creating clarity and why. If school leaders are going to codify their culture, they need to prioritise what will have the greatest impact – and how they will communicate and quality assure the codification.

In *Building Culture* Lekha Sharma (2023) states that "a clear sense of purpose can anchor school improvement efforts" and that "having absolute clarity about our collective purpose in schools means that every single person within a school community is moving in the same direction". Interestingly, Sharma explores clarity of culture and consistent practices so that organisations have a clarity regarding "how we do things around here", or, as Sharma calls it "social norms". These social norms can only become part of the fabric of an organisation – and be part of its improvement – if there is complete alignment from all staff (and a willingness of leaders to not tolerate behaviours that damage these norms). Coyle, in *The Culture Code* (2019), explores a similar concept stating the need to overcommunicate expectations. In his research, he found that successful organisations "were explicit and persistent about sending big, clear signals that established those expectations, modelled cooperation, and aligned language and roles to maximise helpful behaviour". In addition to this, Coyle believes that leaders should be "ten times as clear about [their] priorities as [they] think [they] should be" – and that this "is not the exception but the rule" – so much so, in fact, that they become "part of the oxygen". We believe that effective school leaders, who are emotionally intelligent and self-aware, ask themselves: are our expectations being met? And if not, what can *we* do to ensure they are? This is ultimately about leaders looking in the mirror not through the window.

Sam Crome in *The Power of Teams* (2023) reveals that "communication within the team arises time and time again as a big factor in a team's effectiveness". Crome also highlights that "communication frequency is not a proxy for effectiveness" and that the quality of communication is far more influential to a team and their performance. Crome helpfully focuses on two types of communication that, alongside energy, engagement, and familiarity, contribute to team cohesion and effectiveness. First, Crome highlights information elaboration, which he defines as "the way you communicate information about the team and its work to team members". Here, we are focusing on the importance of delivering clarity in our communication of deadlines, projects, etc. The second type is knowledge sharing, which Crome defines as "how the team exchanges knowledge and expertise so it learns and grows together, pooling its resources". In our experience of leading schools, we believe that leaders should often think about – and look to improve – how they communicate with their team and staff body – it isn't something that happens by chance. Establishing a robust feedback loop after meetings will ensure that each member presenting will continually improve. We believe that school leaders should plan for and differentiate between the two types of communication highlighted by Crome. When leaders have established trusting, vulnerable teams with a clear vision the team becomes accountable to each other for sharing knowledge, deadlines, and project completion, and the team becomes self-regulating. Leaders can use the power of the team to change the team.

> **KEY TAKEAWAYS**
>
> - Creating clarity is the responsibility of leaders. When there is a lack of alignment, leaders should look within their own practice.
> - Leaders must repeatedly communicate their vision and purpose to the people they lead with clarity.
> - Leaders create social norms within their organisations when expectations are communicated with clarity.
> - Clarity of communication within a team can ensure the team are engaged, energetic, and high-performing.

> Elliot is pleased that the school has a secure vision and as he enters his final term of the academic year the school is improving and this is confirmed by both peer visits and external reviews. Elliot is also aware, however, that he has yet to provide full clarity of expectations around aspects of the school. Elliot understands that he achieves the current level of compliance by modelling the behaviour expected – or by brief explanations

in staff meetings and student assemblies. He has built the trust and support of staff that allow him to hold others to account.

He must now spend the time, and it will be considerable, to provide clarity and to codify the culture around the expectations of how he wants things "to be done" at the school. He must also consider which areas to codify first and how many areas need this clarity.

With the support of her headteacher, Amara now understands why she needs to codify the culture within her department. She understands that just explaining at a department meeting what she wants to happen does not provide the long-term clarity for her staff team. They all want both her and the department to do well for the children they serve. Amara is also aware that she needs to identify what areas need codifying first, but is intelligently working with the head of science to share this workload. The departments are geographically based in the same area of school so alignment between these departments is natural and will help both achieve more quicker.

Amara is also aware that she wants all the departments to contribute and is using sightlines to identify which areas to codify first and has run this with both the English and science department together, and this proved very beneficial (Figure 4.1).

Marco has been busy collecting staff, children, and community voices. He has correlated the main themes and presented them to governors. He now needs to codify the behaviour he expects at the school – from both children and adults. He wants to ensure that both well-established and recently appointed staff have real clarity over expectations. He knows that the senior leadership team must all align and put these actions into practice – every day – relentlessly – without fail. If one member of the school team doesn't understand or decides not to put these actions into practice 100% of the time it will jeopardise the whole two terms' work, and he will be back to walking towards his computer fearful of opening his mailbox.

Marco prepares videos so that his staff can see and understand his expectations regarding behaviour expectations – he does this so part-time staff and those new to the school can always access the videos. This codifies expectations of staff and how Marco wants them all to consistently manage behaviour in the corridors, the playground, the classroom, the toilets, and at arrival to school and departure from school. These are the tights of the process that Marco has created – this does not remove staff autonomy or their own personality – rather it empowers staff. Marco does the same for the children at the school and also creates videos for parents and for upcoming and future open evenings. He knows that newsletters are often not read by his community (and, in fact, this can even alienate pockets of his community who have low literacy) but with his relationships with parents the evenings he puts on have great attendance. Marco also runs sessions at a local community centre for parents that never enjoyed school; these parents and carers never engaged before as they often felt talked at and the negative nature of their own schooling was corrosive and bruising. The community centre, with free refreshments – but only a five-minute walk from the school – felt different for them and they comfortably and enthusiastically engaged in a way they hadn't before.

At the start of the next term the school will be spending the first week teaching positive behaviour to the children at the school, and they need to understand the why. All lessons will be on positive behaviour for learning – some staff are worried about the lost learning. Marco is confident that this **is** learning and the time gained for the rest of the academic year and beyond will far outweigh the cost. Staff come to speak with Marco to explain that they have planned their teaching for the academic year and again stress their concerns over lost learning time.

With this in mind, what purposeful steps can Elliot, Amara, and Marco take – and other leaders in similar positions – to create clarity in all that they do?

Figure 4.1 Clarity – Amara

1. **Communicating with clarity**: avoid overwhelming your staff with too many words. Too much information can be just as confusing as too little.

    a. Leaders need absolute certainty around the priorities or messages their staff need to hear. Write down the exact message you need your staff to hear. This can be done in isolation – or with your team.

    b. Ensure that your messaging is consistent across different channels to avoid confusion and maintain clarity.

    c. Plan and rehearse your messaging – and encourage others to do the same. Make rehearsal a normal way of practising key messages to create confidence, alignment, and clarity.

    d. Important messages and priorities should be communicated repeatedly – and in various forms – sometimes every day. Your aim is to ensure the priorities and messages become part of the fabric of your team and school. When you start to hear the correct message being communicated about by other members of staff, you know you've been clear enough.

e. Just like we do in the classroom, summarise and check for understanding. Have your staff heard the message you intended to deliver? And how do you know?

2. **Seeking clarification**: as a leader, there will be times when you lack the clarity you need from others – or need to support colleagues to communicate more precisely and coherently. As a leader, it is important to model how to seek clarification.

   a. Admit unfamiliarity if the discussion or idea is unclear to you. This models vulnerability to those you lead; we don't know everything and it is ok to reveal this. You could ask your colleagues: *I'm unfamiliar with this concept/term. Could you explain what it means?*

   b. Ask for a key message or idea to be repeated if necessary: *could I ask you to repeat your message so that I have the clarity I need?*

   c. Request clarification – ask for more details or a different/simpler explanation: *I'm not sure I've got the clarity I need, could you explain that again?*

   d. Paraphrase by repeating what you think you heard – in your own words to confirm your understanding: *so, if I understand correctly, you're saying that...?*

   e. Summarise and confirm the key points and ask if your understanding is correct: *to summarise, you're suggesting that... Is that right?*

3. **Codification**: leaders might choose to codify a common approach or system. It is important to recognise that this does not remove autonomy or agency – codifying practice in schools can free up cognitive space for teachers and leaders – as well as creating a shortcut, making frequent actions habitual and routine.

   a. Identify an area that would benefit from becoming more consistent or aligned – this is where your efforts will be most rewarded. Aim to triangulate evidence to ensure you're not relying on bias to make a decision: what do learning walks tell you? What does staff voice tell you? What does student voice tell you?

   b. Remain outward-facing. What does the research suggest about this element of practice? What are other schools doing? Make evidence-informed decisions about the codification.

   c. Share the codified area with staff *during its development* so they can all contribute (this might also include student, governor, and other key stakeholder voices). Ask your staff: *why is it important that we have alignment with this?*

Does this codify all aspects or is there still space for confusion?

    d. Ensure that the codified behaviour is recorded down and is accessible. This could be communicated with stakeholders via a variety of methods, e.g. written, video, podcast.

    e. Allocate clear timelines for the codified behaviour, how long will this be in place before a possible review is held. We should all be brave enough to review decisions made but organisations do not benefit from continual change around a process.

4. **Celebrate wins**: precise and sincere recognition and praise is a powerful motivator – boosting engagement and cohesion. Leaders can create a culture of appreciation and respect by recognising and rewarding what they want repeating.

    a. When you witness staff aligning with the agreed clarity ensure it's recognised. Quick "thank you" conversations to staff are often long remembered.

    b. Spotlight staff and ask them to share their success stories with the staff. This voice is often more powerful than the same message from senior leaders each week.

    c. Leadership teams often celebrate staff achievements at the end of the week, ensure that you include those staff that are aligning with the agreed codified behaviours. Senior leaders should be looking and recognising these daily.

    d. Postcards sent home to thank staff are again a positive way to celebrate their efforts. This also provides the staff member with private thanks so they know they are being recognised away from the busy staffroom celebrations on a Friday morning (as much as we like a "thank you it's Friday!" celebration).

    e. Weekly updates to key stakeholders can be shared electronically to share success stories. More schools are now using software such as Stream to develop attractive and engaging communication.

5. **Create clarity of thinking with the sightline process (see appendix)**: In our experience it is best to commence sightlines with senior leaders/heads of department/year leads first. Once this is embedded it naturally flows into other areas of school as staff witness its effectiveness.

    a. Select a problem of practice that you feel would benefit from the collective intelligence of a group, e.g. senior leadership team.

b. Use the timings of the sightline presentation to open your problem of practice (see appendix).

c. Ensure that one member of the team is the moderator (not the presenter). This person must keep to the times and ensure colleagues adhere to the parameters of the section, e.g. for step two when opening a sightline member only seek clarity from the presenter and must not provide advice.

d. Closing a sightline is a shorter process. Make sure all sightlines opened are closed. We advise setting these dates at the start of the academic year or during each term. We are always driving improvements and we always value collective intelligence; in our experience you will have times when you have multiple areas that would benefit from a sightline and the difficulty is choosing just one!

e. Sightlines have to be granular and should be able to be closed within a six- to eight-week window. If you can't, your sightline is too big. Break the boulders into pebbles and then break the pebbles down to sand – this is the right size. For example, you can't address whole school attendance rates in a sightline, but you could focus on a small group of children and see if your sightline creates improvements.

References

Coyle, D. (2019) *The Culture Code.* Random House Publishing.
Crome, S. (2023) *The Power of Teams: How to Create and Lead Thriving School Teams.* John Catt Educational, Limited.
Lencioni, P. (2012) *The Advantage. Why Organisational Health Trumps Everything Else in Business.* Jossey-Bass.
Sharma, L. (2023) *Building Culture. A Handbook to Harnessing Human Nature to Create Strong School Teams.* John Catt Educational Ltd.

Accountability

What does the research tell us?

In 2017 Lane conducted a study to identify brain signals that explain why our self-esteem rises, or lowers, when we find out what others think of us. The study saw participants receive feedback from strangers based on an online profile – they were either liked or disliked. The study revealed that when people had increased prediction error responses (the difference between expected and actual feedback) in a part of the brain called the insula, there was greater activity in the prefrontal cortex that explained changes in self-esteem. What this tells us about accountability is leaders must understand the power they hold over those they lead. In 2020, Ron Carucci explores the findings of this study stating that leaders must make "dignity the foundation" and that leaders should "believe their role is to create conditions in which people make their best contributions – and genuinely enjoy doing so". Carucci believes that when leaders believe this, accountability begins to deepen connections between leaders and direct reports and the quality of feedback and learning increases. It is our belief that school leaders always leave a wake with each interaction they make, that is why it's important that the recipient of the conversation feels genuinely heard. This does not mean agreeing with each colleague of course – disagreement can be healthy for an organisation with the correct conditions.

Lencioni (2012) believes that "peer-to-peer accountability is the primary and most effective source of accountability on the leadership team of a healthy organisation". Lencioni goes on to consider that in some unhealthy and noncohesive organisations, one person is predominantly responsible for holding colleagues to account – often the leader. Lencioni suggests that this model is inefficient and impractical – and it makes little sense. We believe that when a school team holds each other to account, for example turning up to staff duty on time to relieve a colleague, then all staff become leaders and that this model will produce the legacy good schools should have to reduce the risk of leadership change.

Interestingly, Lencioni also explores the fact that the only way for a team to develop a true culture of peer-to-peer accountability "is for the leader to demonstrate that she is willing to confront difficult situations and hold people accountable...the leader of the team, though not the primary source of accountability, will always be the ultimate arbiter of it". School staff look at leadership teams for the culture of a school, if a headteacher releases a policy or an assembly stating that X will happen if Y occurs but the ground truth is they don't follow this through, don't expect others at school to do so. They will become disillusioned, lower standards or leave.

To be a great school leader, we need to get good at delivering information that helps our colleagues improve – like Brene Brown (2019) says: "clear is kind". Lencioni thinks that "at its core, accountability is about having the courage to confront someone about their deficiencies and then to stand in the moment and deal with their reaction...it is a selfless act". Without trust this can be very challenging, but it's important to consider that the reaction of a colleague is a reflection of them and not you. In *Time to Think* Rachel Johnson (2023) explores how to overcome people-pleasing tendencies, highlighting that people-pleasing can prevent you from giving feedback to a colleague because "you don't want to say what needs to be said because you don't want to feel their disapproval". We believe that this will be detrimental to the school and its community; disapproval may need to be felt to drive the school to where it needs to be. This idea is reinforced in Lekha Sharma's *Building Culture* (2023). Sharma suggests that one of the ways school leaders can build a culture of continuous improvement is "giving feedback that is sometimes uncomfortable to give but will have a major impact on the practice of those we lead".

In *Fierce Leadership*, Susan Scott (2011) believes that "next to human connectivity, accountability is the single most powerful, most desired, yet least understood characteristic of a successful human being and a successful environment". She goes on to suggest that the phrase "fierce accountability" might, initially, seem frightening or even aggressive to some – yet:

> if you think of *fierce* in the most positive light, like fierce loyalty, fierce resolve, or fierce friendship, you might associate fierce accountability with a bias towards action and passionate commitment to exceptional results, even in the face of obstacles.

Often this is the most challenging area for recently appointed leaders, especially those promoted from within. Our advice is to role-play the conversation with another leader at the school, and such deliberate practice really can prove beneficial.

In *Intelligent Accountability*, David Didau (2020) explores whole school accountability processes; stating "the biggest mistake we make when holding teachers (or anyone else) to account is telling them what "right" looks like before the process begins". Didau goes on to suggest three ways that accountability can become intelligent:

1. Teachers know how they will be held accountable before judgements are made; 2. The views of the people holding teachers to account are unknown; 3. Teachers believe that those holding them to account are well informed and interested in accuracy.

The use of solution-focused coaching can reduce the need for leaders to simply jump in with suggestions and answers but allows for a two-way conversation over what "better" might look like.

> **KEY TAKEAWAYS**
>
> - Accountability will leave an emotional wake – this doesn't have to be a negative thing. Done well, accountability can be a joy.
> - Peer-to-peer accountability is considered one of the most effective accountability models in an organisation – particularly over a model which predominantly relies on one person to hold others to account.
> - Leaders need to put courage over comfort (Brene Brown).

Elliot is pleased with the impact on the school that both he and the staff have made; he is confident the school is improving and he continues to model the culture he expects. The lead for teaching and learning has worked diligently on codifying the expectations within the classroom and a consistent approach can be seen from classroom visits. Elliot believes that by creating this level of codification it will reduce cognitive load for children moving from class to class and each step has always been based on research. Some staff have pushed back that it is taking away their autonomy in the classroom but Elliot has been careful not to turn each class into some kind of franchise; personalities are clear in the classrooms and children enjoy the learning.

Behaviour is good and whilst this has not needed the amount of codification teaching and learning required, the interactions between staff and children are always positive and recently appointed staff quickly align to this culture. The school is caring and well supported, perhaps the catchment area helps with this, and deprivation is low.

However, feedback from his teaching and learning lead is that in certain classrooms staff expectations are not being met. She feels when she arrives the teacher will simply move into a list of things to do because of her presence. Talk to your partner – tick, use of whiteboards – tick, adaptive teaching – tick. Elliot needs to unpick this, if this is true it's a challenge to the school expectations. As a new head he seeks advice from an experienced head. He must hold these staff members to account, if he doesn't the staff will know and he will feel as though he is letting down the other teachers working hard to improve outcomes.

Amara has worked with the head of science at the school to clarify expectations at their department meetings. The head of science has shared that during her meetings, staff will often display body language that she feels is negative to ideas that a newly appointed second in science suggests. Certain staff fold their arms and lean back on their seats when she talks; at other times they will just check-out of the conversations when she asks for suggestions from them. Amara suggests that they could hold joint meetings at times of the year when working on shared areas such as teaching and learning or behaviour. The head of science agrees, but is worried that the behaviour shown at the science meeting might spread into the English department if they are given free reign of how to behave.

Marco is really pleased with the first week back at school. He had ensured that during the first week back he was walking the corridors (Figure 5.1) to ensure that staff had the correct lesson on the screen – he had colour-coded the background to the slides so it was a quick task. All the staff have shown the presentations he had prepared regarding positive behaviour for learning in their lessons, the feedback from the community was positive, and his headteacher had thanked him publicly in the staff meeting for all his efforts. Marco had chatted to children at the school and they had all heard the same messages about the why – it was because the school cared for them and wanted them to succeed in life – Marco was feeling positive and proud.

March has been at the school for several years, and as the only consistent member of the senior leadership team, the staff had often confided in him and trusted him with their concerns and beliefs. He understood that he had to hold all staff to account for the new behaviour system. This could be a challenge for him. He wanted to be visible and not in his office behind a closed door. Whilst all staff were responsible for the new system he was the flag bearer, leading from the front. As he walked the corridor he held every member of staff to account. If they ignored children not following the rules he would step in, ask to borrow the children, and model the language he expected. It felt awkward at first, but it soon became normal and the staff expected him to do this. His next step was ensuring that the staff held each other to account, that was when he felt he could feel satisfied. The senior leadership team met each morning to ensure that any issues that arose could be solved so that in every staff and student interaction you couldn't see any light between them.

Of course it had challenging moments, some children pushed against the expectations, and that led to sanctions, but the change was already being felt by the school community and there would be no backing down now. The tightness of the senior leadership team meant that the staff trusted that no secret deals with parents would be done. They were certain that they could stand with the behaviour policy without fear of leaders stepping back from it. This trust was essential in driving improvements at the school.

However, some parents had become aggressive stating that their children would not be "doing any sanctions" and that the school was "becoming like a prison camp". Marco knew this wasn't the case, the children and staff felt much happier, and these parents had never engaged or visited the school, but what should he do now?

With this in mind, what purposeful steps can Elliot, Amara, and Marco take – and other leaders in similar positions – to embrace and encourage accountability?

Figure 5.1 Accountability – Marco

1. **Think about accountability**: first, consider what it is that you want accountability to achieve for your organisation and what might happen if accountability is not established. Who is responsible for accountability at the organisation and how do you know that it is or isn't happening?

    a. Talk and think about accountability: thinking and talking about accountability will influence our beliefs and change our behaviour in our own context and with the people in it. Talk to your team about accountability in your organisation – make it a comfortable conversation: Are there pockets of high-impact accountability that are really making a difference? Are there any spaces in school free from any level of accountability – and what is the impact of this?

    b. Self-accountability: consider how robustly you hold yourself to account for leading through your values and ethos – never losing sight of what you stand for. There will be times in schools when the only person to hold you accountable and responsible is yourself. These moments are where school leaders could take the easier pathway and not one that benefits children the most – these are the moments when you need to hold fast to your beliefs and never lower your standards.

    c. Disrupt your own thinking about accountability: often leaders can hold a negative view of accountability – based on their own experiences. There are leaders who can destroy your sense of worth and confidence by getting accountability wrong and instead unfairly criticising and demoralising you. There are also leaders whose unwavering belief in you can make you better by holding you to account fairly and robustly – because better is possible with accountability.

d. Consider how you receive accountability: as a leader, it is important to model to your team how you openly seek and receive accountability. Coyle (2019) suggests we should hug the messenger believing that "one of the most vital moments for creating safety is when a group shares bad news or gives tough feedback. In these moments, it's important not simply to tolerate the difficult news but to embrace it" we have to "let them know how much you need that feedback. That way you can be sure that they feel safe enough to tell you the truth next time".

e. Levels of accountability: as a leader in your organisation, you need to have clear expectations around the accountability you desire and these expectations should be overcommunicated – without this, you leave colleagues feeling unfairly exposed and susceptible to unjust challenge.

2. **Talk about accountability**: Great leaders hold others to account when it is what is right for the organisation. And holding staff to account isn't something you're either good or bad at – it is a leadership habit that can be learnt. Talk to your staff about accountability – unpick their thinking and experiences of accountability.

a. Communicate the importance: explain why accountability is crucial for the team's success. Highlight how it contributes to achieving goals, maintaining trust, and fostering a positive and high-performing environment.

b. Set clear expectations: begin by clearly outlining what is expected from each team member. Define roles and responsibilities. Perhaps even consider rehearsing an example so as to avoid the knowing-doing gap.

c. Encourage open dialogue: create a safe space where team members feel comfortable discussing the progress and successes – as well as the challenges they're experiencing with accountability. Encourage them to ask questions and share feedback, which can help identify and address potential issues early on.

d. Provide support and resources: ensure your team has the necessary tools, training, and support to meet their accountability responsibilities. Offer guidance and assistance when needed to help them succeed. If you can observe them holding others to account, you can give precise and useful feedback.

e. Follow-up and review: regularly check in on progress – perhaps consider making it an agenda item (either formally or informally). Recognise achievements and address any lapses in accountability promptly and fairly. This helps reinforce the importance of accountability and encourages continuous improvement – because everyone can be better.

3. **How to encourage accountability at all levels – create a Probletunity Group**: it is important that you foster a culture where all staff are able to hold each other to account; whilst it stops with the headteacher, they alone cannot hold the whole organisation to account. Finding times to help others find comfort and joy in accountability will benefit the school. Creating a Probletunity Group will empower staff to hold leaders to account and provide solutions to issues perhaps not recognised by senior leaders (see the appendix for Probletunity form template).

    a. Invite representative staff from every area of school (teachers, premises, catering, office, etc.) and ensure they all feel welcome to share a Probletunity. Create a consistent time and space every week which means staff are able to attend, and feel safe to be honest and constructive. In our experience these meetings should not last longer than 30 minutes and the initial meets will most likely have more items to cover, and consider spreading these out over the first few weeks. In many ways this is good news as you are mining new areas for issues with solutions.

    b. Norms and contracting: outline and establish the norms – the accepted behaviours and rules that govern all interactions within the Probletunity Group. This will create safety for all members. Consider who you want to be the chair and vice chair of the meeting. In our experience we never chaired the group as heads of school; in many cases we asked a newly qualified teacher if they would be one of the group leads.

    c. How to run a meeting: staff should arrive at the meeting with a problem of practice and an opportunity that could improve the situation – a "Probletunity" (see appendix). All items added to the agenda must have a Probletunity form submitted at least 48 hours before the meeting. These should be shared with all the staff involved to allow consideration and careful thought prior to the meeting.

    d. Things to say in the first (and subsequent) meetings to deliver safety cues: depending on your leadership role within your school, it may be useful for you to deliver frequent and consistent safety cues (see overcommunicate your listening in **Trust** for more; see Chapter 1). Alternatively, it may be more useful for you to say very little.

    e. Follow-up: it is important that, where appropriate, the members of the Probletunity Group see that their time and effort have created meaningful action. At times, this needs to be narrated to them – not all action taken in schools is obvious or visible.

4. **Practise accountability**: it is important to rehearse holding others to account. To get great at holding people to account you have to hold people to account.

a. Script it: prepare some notes and key phrases ahead of the conversation so that you have clarity over the message that you want to deliver.

b. Rehearse it: role-play the conversation with a trusted colleague before you hold the real conversation. Do this until you are confident your message will be delivered clearly.

c. Feedback: during the rehearsal ensure that the message you wish to deliver is being heard – ask your trusted colleague what they have heard and what you could have done better.

d. Deliver: take your notes with you and stay on script so the message has the clarity that you achieved during the rehearsal.

e. Debrief: talk to your trusted colleague about how the delivery went. Are there areas you wished had been clearer? Do you feel more confident in your ability to provide this feedback? Is there any action you need to commit to help in future deliveries?

5. **Accountability mechanisms**: school leaders will want to establish and run a range of accountability systems to ensure that all staff have access to helpful and positive feedback, which helps them grow and get better. Intelligent accountability should be informed by the collection of a reliable range of data collection and research – both internal school data and external good practice.

    a. Establish effective Line Management systems at all levels: Create a common agenda for all Line Management schedules which are published at the start of the year, with standing items such as leadership development, which both parties can contribute to ahead of the meeting – ensuring that accountability is visible and consistent. At Headteacher and Trust level, leaders may want to develop a system to ensure Line Management is happening routinely in schools.

    b. Lesson visits: the name of these is not that really important; what is important is how we collect information from these visits and act on the findings. A timely feedback mechanism should be established. The Senior Leadership Team regularly discusses Teaching and Learning across the school – and agrees actions to tackle areas of improvement.

    c. Curriculum planning: how are you ensuring that your lead on curriculum knows that the intended curriculum is being taught in the classrooms? Ensure your systems enable you to make informed decisions about the quality of the curriculum planning and that the curriculum is viable for the space given, and that all children will have access to it.

    d. Behaviour: how is data being collected so that you can teach students the gaps in their knowledge. These areas could involve how children are keeping the canteen clean and walking along the corridors respectfully, or their use of appropriate language for example. This data should be discussed with year/house staff, senior leaders, and governors – with agreed actions and timelines.

e. Attendance: how do you ensure that the senior lead for attendance has the data required to be accountable for this portfolio area? How do you collect data about groups of students and indeed the students that individually sit within each group? What data packages can you adopt to help? This data should be shared on regular occasions so that you are all accountable for it. Nothing is more important than ensuring the children are with you each day if you are to improve life chances.

References

Brown, B. (2019) *Dare to Lead*. Random House Publishing.

Carucci, R. (2020) "How to actually encourage employee accountability." *Harvard Business Review*, https://hbr.org/2020/11/how-to-actually-encourage-employee-accountability. Accessed 7 July 2024.

Coyle, D. (2019) *The Culture Code*. Random House Publishing.

Didau, D. (2020) *Intelligent Accountability: Creating the Conditions for Teachers to Thrive*. John Catt.

Johnson, R. (2023) *Time to Think: The Things that Stop Us and How to Deal with Them*. John Catt.

Lane, C. (2017) "Self esteem mapped in the human brain." *Neuroscience News*, https://neurosciencenews.com/self-esteem-brain-mapping-7799/. Accessed 7 July 2024.

Lencioni, P. (2012) *The Advantage. Why Organisational Health Trumps Everything Else in Business*. Jossey-Bass.

Scott, S. (2011) *Fierce Leadership: A Bold Alternative to the Worst 'Best Practices' of Business Today*. Piatkus.

Sharma, L. (2023) *Building Culture: A Handbook to Harnessing Human Nature to Create Strong School Teams*. John Catt.

6 Adaptability

What does the research tell us?

Daniel Goleman, in his book *Leadership That Gets Results* (2000), outlines six distinct leadership styles that leaders tend to use. From our experience leaders do tend to favour some styles over others – but all can be useful at different times. Leaders should consider the impact of each style on the people being led and on the climate of the school. In *Leadership Matters*, Andy Buck (2018) asks "do you make a conscious effort to think about the right approach for any given situation or do you rely on gut instinct?".

Authoritative (visionary) leaders have a clear and compelling dream of the future, and they know how to communicate it. A large school community may not always agree on every direction a leader sets but they can buy into the preferred future for all. We also understand that just a dream with no direction of how to get there can be hollow words and staff quickly become disillusioned. It is no good being a visionary leader with no map to arrive at the dream.

Coaching leaders encourage continuous learning and employee engagement, contributing to long-term organisational success. Coaching leaders take time and effort; it's often quicker to let colleagues know what it is that you want them to do, but this could stifle them of their own professional development, and quality time with you as a leader that they will value.

Affiliative leaders prioritise team harmony by building strong relationships, fostering belongingness, and creating a supportive work atmosphere. They focus on open communication, empathy, and trust to resolve conflicts and enhance team cohesion. As a leader you are in a privileged position, and we have mentioned earlier that leaders create a wake when they walk down a school corridor; what wake can you leave behind to help develop strong relationships? In our experience helping a colleague struggling to fix a photocopier, greeting staff by their names, and making them feel like their conversation is important to you as opposed to thinking, because it states Principal on your door, you are more important than others are essential.

Democratic leaders involve team members in decision-making processes, valuing their input and fostering a collaborative culture. We believe that autonomy is a large factor of job satisfaction and in some schools we can see this being eroded away with staff. As a result our most creative work colleagues leave to seek alternative workplaces and the organisation suffers longer term. How do you provide a voice for others to make suggestions and raise issues with the workplace or do you hide away from this due to believing that you must know all the answers or due to insecurity? How does the whole school community bring problems but with suggested solutions to the table? Collective intelligence is much more powerful, and empowering for staff, than a done to you approach. We believe that a true leader that removes the mask of invisibility will have greater long-term success.

Pacesetting leaders set high standards and expect their team to meet them, inspiring excellence through role modelling. While effective in the short term, this style may limit creativity and autonomy in the long run, emphasising the need for appropriate support alongside challenges. This is when we need to lean into the democratic leadership style to ensure creativity and autonomy still exist. As leaders we all have times when we just need to get multiple areas developed and developed quickly, e.g. when you take on a school that is failing. That said we don't believe that distributed leadership or collective intelligence leads to dithering over decisions; it can be achieved rapidly with the correct timelines attached.

Directive leaders assert immediate compliance through a top-down, direct approach. While effective in crises, overuse of this style can create a negative work environment, potentially impeding employee engagement and creativity. We have witnessed this leadership in schools before; it can provide quick wins and short-term gain but ultimately we always see eventual staff dissatisfaction and staff leaving. Who wants to run an organisation with staff counting down the years until their retirement when just a few years earlier they were the staff driving the school forwards?

Each leadership style has its strengths and weaknesses, and effective leaders are often able to adapt their approach depending on the situation and the needs of their team. Goleman suggests that a blend of these styles, known as "Primal Leadership", is most effective for inspiring and motivating teams to achieve their goals. Buck suggests that "taking a moment to think about your leadership approach, and, in particular, the right style for your situation, has the potential to make a big difference to the discretionary effort in your team".

The conscious decision to adopt certain leadership styles to suit varying contexts and people requires cognitive space. When school leaders are stressed and under pressure, they will not have the cognitive capacity to adapt – they will rely on ingrained habits and behaviours that have served them so far. This raises interesting questions about experience and expertise. In *Leadership for Teacher Learning*, Dylan Wiliam (2016) highlights that in many areas "performance declines with experience". It is clear that if we hope to move towards leadership expertise, experience is a necessary condition – but not a sufficient condition. We believe that in order to move towards leadership expertise, leaders must consciously choose to grow and learn.

Wiliam states that experts "perceive more meaningful patterns in what they observe" – they look at patterns and rhythms – rather than individual stand-alone moments. In school leadership, this could possibly mean that expert leaders create stronger and more durable schemas – William states the "difference between experts and novices is not so much in the amount of knowledge but how it is organised". This ability to make connections and "inter-relations also helps experts remember details of related situations". This allows school leaders to make intelligent decisions and adapt accordingly. School leaders can begin to do this once they are able to automate basic routines – therefore not using up precious and very limited cognitive capacity.

A growing body of research suggests that in order to move purposefully towards expertise, deliberate practice is necessary. This is where our book can help you!

We believe that you need to be authentic to the type of leader you truly are, and you will always fit naturally into one of the leadership styles above. Other styles can be developed, and we have witnessed this, but ask staff, and they will most likely predominantly put their leader into one of the categories above. Really think deeply about what it is you want to achieve and how you think you are best suited to arrive there; if you are authentic the mask will never fall – you won't need one.

When confronted with highly stressful circumstances, we can experience a narrowing of vision and a fixation solely on threats. This tunnel vision obscures everything else, directing our efforts and energy towards our fears or concerns. Facing stressful and unknown experiences at school is frequent – because of the nature of our work with young people (and staff) – there are moments throughout our career for which we don't have a strong mental model. During these times, leaders can respond in a maladaptive way. In "Situation Awareness, understanding what it happened in order to act" Jennfier Delgado believes that "when we go through complex times marked by change and uncertainty, we need a special psychological tool: situational awareness". Situational awareness is the ability to perceive, comprehend, and anticipate events and circumstances in one's surroundings, enabling informed decision-making and effective responses. Delgado goes on to suggest that situational awareness is:

> knowing what is going on around us. It involves drawing a kind of mental map that helps us understand where we are, what surrounds us and what are the challenges that lie ahead. This ability allows us to see clearly what is happening to develop an effective coping plan.

School leaders face unanticipated and fresh challenges on a daily basis; experience allows us to link past knowledge to new but different challenges so that we can adapt plans to fit. The impact of a global pandemic on schools and the ability of leaders across the world to create coping plans demonstrates the ability of our education leaders in times of complex uncertainty.

> **KEY TAKEAWAYS**
>
> - It is important to be flexible and adaptable in your response to situational and contextual awareness.
> - School leaders should consider which leadership style is their preferred style – knowing that, at times, all styles could be appropriate and effective.
> - Situational awareness will enable school leaders to look up and gain some distance during stressful and unknown circumstances in order to respond and adapt.

Elliot is proud of how he has developed collective intelligence using mainly a democratic leadership style at the school. He has no doubt that this is helping to improve the life chances of his students. Elliot is also sure that this leadership style is developing staff satisfaction with low levels of staff turnover and high scores for job satisfaction from his staff surveys. Elliot knows the names of all his co-workers, and he doesn't like to call them employees. If the school is not clean or the food is not served the organisation suffers; everyone is important. Elliot knows they all have a part to play to reach the vision for the school. He has created new ways to collect co-worker thoughts and recently launched "probletunity" with his staff to further the collective intelligence (see appendix). His head of English is not sure of the name but appreciates what it will bring to the school (Figure 6.1).

Amara has held meetings with both the English and science departments. She clarified the expectations for the meeting so everyone is clear. Whilst the English department is always keen to use collective intelligence to make the decisions that will benefit the children and department most, it became clear that some of her science department colleagues often checked out. Whilst Amara believes in staff working together she is strong to hold others to account. She often has to lean into the directive leadership approach to ensure that she holds the teams to account. She cannot afford for meetings to drift and for unfelt emotions to continue to fester, which benefits no one. Amara moves into a variety of leadership styles to suit the situation whilst always being aware that is fair and honest with all the staff that she manages – this takes skill as a leader can fall into certain styles based on relationships.

Marco continues to develop the behaviour for learning model at the school and the school staff and governors are full of praise for the work he has done. However, having long-standing relationships with staff can bring challenges to him. He has naturally grown close to some of his colleagues, some staff members he meets outside school to play football with. It's also a challenge to them as Marco continues to have a large influence on the school and its expectations. One member of staff is well liked by colleagues and children; his roots run deep at the school. However, Marco also knows that at times this colleague leaves the school site early and does not always follow the behaviour expectations at the school. His headteacher has asked Marco to hold him to account, and Marco understands that his behaviours are not fair to his colleagues but this will be a challenge to him.

With this in mind, what purposeful steps can Elliot, Amara, and Marco take – and other leaders in similar positions – to adapt and flex?

Figure 6.1 Adaptability – Elliot

1. **Think about your leadership style**: often time allows us to consider which leadership style will be best for certain situations – sometimes school leaders are unprepared and enter a situation blind. Using your emotional intelligence should guide you. And we can't be all things to all people.

    a. Reflect: consider the leaders who you've been your best with – what did this look like? What leadership style gave you the freedom and space to be your best? Consider the leaders who left you uninspired, lacking in confidence, close to breaking. Learn from all these experiences, and they are valuable in informing you of how you want to lead your team.

    b. Judgement: whilst we appreciate that not all situations can be rehearsed in schools we believe in the importance of deliberately mental modelling whenever possible. Model the meeting with a trusted colleague or visualise it; identify the leadership style that will move you closer to the desired outcome.

    Re-check during the meeting that you are not being pulled away from the style you desire; keep a check on your emotions.

    As your experience grows your judgement on which leadership style is most effective in situations develops. Initially, use time to consider the planned meeting ahead, what is it you want your staff to feel, and what is it you need to achieve. Not all meetings can be prepared for, and many can be ad-hoc as you walk the corridor or a colleague arrives at your door, but you should always have time to recentre yourself before you commence the conversation.

c. Schemas/patterns: purposefully look for connections and patterns in interactions during the school day – and deliberately create mental models of what works – and possibly, what doesn't. There are important day-to-day tasks which leaders can automate to conserve cognitive capacity. Causal reasoning tells us that often when situations arise there follows a pattern of events: when we do A, B is likely to happen. Identify these patterns in your school – what can we learn from this?

d. Talk about leadership adaptability: talk to your team about leadership adaptability – make it a comfortable conversation. Is there a dichotomy between the leadership style you perceive you are exhibiting and what your colleagues believe to be your dominant leadership style? Make it a safe conversation – ask for feedback.

e. North Star: think deeply about who you really are and what you stand for: who do you want to be? What type of school do you want to lead? The answers to these questions, which won't necessarily be easy to find, will become your North Star: stay true to this. Choosing to behave in a way which undermines your North Star will create cognitive dissonance and it is not a sustainable way to lead.

2. **Keep your leadership style in check**: keep your emotions in check during conversations – we always want to demonstrate respect, and, where possible, lead deliberately and purposefully. There will naturally be times when your emotions compete with your planned, deliberate leadership style. We cannot – and shouldn't – suppress our emotions, but we can control them. Carla Naumburg's Mindful S.N.A.C.K. (2016) is a useful tool for school leaders to increase awareness:

a. STOP: at times, it can feel difficult to stop or pause. Naumburg states: "stopping, by definition, requires us to begin again", and we can often begin again with more skill and more effectiveness after a moment's break. Put down your pen, move away from your desk, or embrace a moment of silence during a conversation.

b. NOTICE: deliberately notice what is happening within and around you. Get to know how your body responds to stress or pressure – and notice it when it begins to occur (perhaps tense shoulders or a shortness of breath). Simply become aware of what is happening – notice but do not judge.

c. ACCEPT: whatever it is you're dealing with – or finding difficult – acknowledge it without judgement, and with the knowledge that some things can't be changed.

d. CURIOUS: Naumburg believes that "the ability to get interested in our experience and environment can help us manage difficult emotions and gain some clarity on what is going on. You don't have to undertake a serious investigation requiring an hour of therapy; a few simple questions should suffice. What am I feeling? What am I thinking? What do I need right now?"

e. KINDNESS: choose to respond to the problem, yourself, and your staff with kindness and notice the power this has on all.

3. **Develop your Situational Awareness**: school leaders' attention and working memory are often critical factors limiting our ability to develop Situational Awareness. Developing Situational Awareness with mental models and goal-oriented behaviours help mitigate against these daily challenges; leading schools is complex and hard – finding ways to develop Situational Awareness can help us adapt more effectively.

   a. Where are you? Carefully consider the environment around you to avoid moving into a state of "situational stupidity". Without this knowledge, we can disconnect from our current situation and instead are motivated by and make adaptations based on bias or fear.

   b. Find meaning: now that you have clarity around where you are, consider how you got there; dig into past experiences to look for patterns or rhythms. Consider what an environmental baseline would look and sound like – the environmental baseline is what you have experienced in similar situations and environments: what is different and/or the same now?

   c. Project: purposefully imagine the desired future state – what obstacles did you have to overcome? What dangers and/or threats got in your way? What action did you take to be successful?

   d. Causal reasoning: identifying causality – the relationship between a cause and its effect can help us better adapt to our situations and contexts. Using knowledge of cause-effect relations, we are able to diagnose and solve problems. When approaching leadership challenges, consider: *might A lead to B? How might A lead to C?*

   e. Fight complacency: school leaders need to fight against comfort and the status quo in order to avoid leading with autopilot on with minimal thinking. Purposefully re-evaluate your situation and environment so as to avoid growing accustomed to it – better is possible!

4. **Adapt to respond to need**: there will always be times in schools when school leaders need to take rapid action to secure improvement – this might be within a small team or at a whole school level. The ability to flex leadership styles to respond to need is a skill any leader can learn.

    a. Situational Awareness: using the steps to develop Situational Awareness, decide why your current situation might require rapid action: what is the immediate threat?

    b. Talk to your staff: communicate clearly to your staff – explaining why you're choosing to adopt a directive and pacesetting leadership style to overcome this current challenge. Remember to communicate the direction and vision and how you're going to get there – and that the intention isn't to choose this style for the long term.

    c. Timescale: a directive and/or pacesetting leadership style is not a sustainable approach and is often not conducive to staff retention and their autonomy. Even during periods of rapid change it is still vital that clear timelines with checkpoints are developed (barring emergencies at school).

    d. Evidence-informed: despite the immediate nature of this current threat or danger in your setting, your leadership actions should be evidence-informed. Don't abdicate your responsibility to make research-led decisions because the situation you're facing is urgent. Slow down to speed up. Hurry slowly.

    e. Adapt again: deliberately move out of the directive leadership style – when you feel secure that the immediate threat has been reduced (or, in fact, removed) consider which approach is a best fit now – and who is best placed to continue its development. It may be that during the initial stages of this rapid improvement, you have taken on sole leadership – this might not be a sustainable approach in the long term.

5. **Debrief**: in order for school leaders to move towards expertise, experience alone is not enough. Reflection and a disposition to learn and improve are also necessary. Carving out time to debrief and evaluate the leadership styles you've chosen to use and the impact this has had on people and systems is essential.

    a. Decide which actions/events you'll reflect on: given the busy nature of schools it would be unrealistic to systematically review and reflect on every decision made. But there will be moments which deserve time and attention. As a school leader you should carefully select the moments within the term that should dedicate structured reflection time to.

    b. Schedule a time to review the following: agenda dedicated time to reflect on your leadership style – consider preparing questions to guide reflection;

this works best when multiple staff are involved so that the perspective is broad.

- *What did you notice about the leadership style I chose to adopt?*
- *What impact did this leadership style have on staff?*
- *How might the overall outcome have been different had I chosen a different leadership style?*

c. Consider how to gain feedback from a wider audience: a 360-degree leadership reflection tool might be useful for school leaders to better understand how their leadership traits are being received by their co-workers. We recommend this is conducted annually at the same point in the school year to allow healthy comparison.

d. Talk to your staff: share your reflections with staff – model the deliberate and thoughtful nature of your leadership choices – look ahead and explain that, at different points of the school's development, different leadership styles will be adopted to create the change required.

e. Better is possible: using the feedback gained – and from your own reflections – which leadership areas could you further strengthen, and how might you go about this? Work with experienced and expert colleagues from within and outside your organisation; read widely; locate training opportunities. Consider what improving in this area would look like in your future leadership reviews – has it made a difference?

References

Buck, A. (2018) *Leadership Matters 3.0: How Leaders at All Levels Can Create Great Schools*. John Catt Educational Limited.

Delgado, J. "Situational awareness, understanding what is happening in order to act." *Psychology Spot*, https://psychology-spot.com/situational-awareness/. Accessed 13 April 2024.

Goleman, D. (2000) *Leadership That Gets Results*. Harvard Business Review.

Goleman, D., Boyatzis, R. and McKee, A. (2002) *Primal Leadership: Unleashing the Power of Emotional Intelligence*. Harvard Business Review Press.

Naumburg, C. (2016) "How to take a mindful S.N.A.C.K. Moment." *Mindful.org*, https://www.mindful.org/how-to-take-mindful-snack/. Accessed 28 July 2024.

Wiliam, D. (2016) *Leadership for Teacher Learning*. Learning Sciences International.

7 Legacy

What does the research tell us?

In *Legacy*, James Kerr (2013) highlights the All Blacks practice of being a good ancestor and planting trees you'll never see. Kerr states that being a good ancestor is caring about "contribution to the lineage of the company and the team, even the planet – and about our contribution as individuals to a deer continuum". The All Blacks call this leaving the jersey in a better place. Kerr goes on to clarify this belief: "it means to be a custodian of the future, an architect of tomorrow, a steward of society. It means to live with respect, humility and excellence". Great leaders should leave great schools behind them, and we believe that hero headteachers who lead on everything and keep a tight grip on all developments can stifle other leaders within the school. They can leave a school for bigger things and the children suffer.

In a similar way, Rachel Johnson dedicates a chapter of *Time to Think* (2023) to explore how school leaders can face the brutal facts and still have unwavering hope. Johnson suggests that leaders should remind people of the end game and keep hope alive. Without hope, what do we have? In times of budget issues, recruitment difficulties, and attendance concerns it can be too easy to lose hope. But we believe that school leaders should continue to have hope for our schools, our staff, and our children – and never lose this.

Mary Myatt in *Hopeful Schools* (2016) believes that school leaders "have stuff to learn from yesterday, both positive and negative. But we only have this moment, now, to live in. And it's a pity if we don't expect and hope for a better world tomorrow". Myatt shares a story of a school turned around by a remarkable leader – the school transformed into an organisation where "there were no passengers. Why? Because one great leader had given them a new story, one they could relate to at the deepest level. That of hope and confidence in the future".

We believe that in order for school leaders to leave a legacy and to leave their school in a better place, they need to be their best more of the time. In *Leadership Plain and Simple*, Steve Radcliffe (2012) believes that "when you're at your most confident best, you're powerfully in touch with the future you want and not held back by the present". Radcliffe goes on to consider that when leaders are "just surviving, your focus is not on the glorious future you want. It's more on "how do I survive now?" There is little sense of energising possibilities". This is when leadership teams become stuck in the operational matters of a school and have little, if any, time to look into the future at what we want the school to become. As each day, week, month, and year passes the school drifts; leadership teams simply survive.

> **KEY TAKEAWAYS**
>
> ▪ Leaving a legacy means working towards a vision and, ultimately, leaving your school in a better place.
> ▪ Leading with unwavering hope ensures the end game is always in sight.
> ▪ It is not always easy for leaders to maintain hope – there will be times when they feel hopeless. Leaders should look ahead to find hope when it feels like it is faltering.

> After four years in post Elliot has been asked if he would be prepared to take on a joint headship across two schools, his current one and a school in a similar catchment area that has declining results and a falling roll. The previous head had left unexpectedly and the school needed leadership. Elliot had read that second headships often fail as often we simply try to replicate what we did at our first school into the second. Often a different community needs a different approach. Elliot had committed four years of his life to improve the school he was working at and now understood the commitment headship takes to make a difference. Would he have the energy to do this again on a part-time basis or would both schools simply suffer due to having less of him at the school? Elliot also thought about why he came to work in schools; it wasn't about headship; it was about making schools better for the children they serve. Elliot was also sure that his current school would function well without him; he has a good deputy head and during his headship he made sure that it wasn't all down to him like some kind of hero head. Elliot spoke with his family, his governors, and the senior leadership team and made the jump.
>
> Amara is pleased with the progression of the English department. The team are aligned and the outcomes for children have steadily improved each year. All the team have stepped up to make the department one of the strongest at the school. At times it's been challenging, but Amara knows that this comes with leadership. She has used the group to make decisions and when alignment could not be found she has decided the course of action that she feels is best for the children. She is very proud of how many children move to post 16 and take A-level English as one of their course choices; this was quite rare just a few years ago. Every September when the headteacher goes over the summer results she feels a great sense of pride.

Within the school some departments are still struggling to improve with outcomes below the national average – some are outliers every results day with the same children performing better in other subjects. In September the headteacher asks to meet with her – he wants her to line manage one of the worst performing subject areas at the school with poor outcomes and children leaving the options group in droves. It's not a subject area she is strong in – but the headteacher explains that it is about leadership and accountability. His plan is to move the second in English to be acting head of department and make her director of faculty across two subject areas. It's a huge compliment but she also knows it will come with issues from the other head of department who has been at the school a long time and is well connected with staff. She is undecided (Figure 7.1).

Marco is proud of his contribution towards the outcomes and safety of the children at his school improving. The staff retention has increased and often when employment opportunities are advertised some of the staff that left due to the behaviour are looking to return. Elliot has no issue with this, and he wants the best teachers in front of the disadvantaged children they serve. Ego has no place with Elliot. Applications for children's places at the school are at an all-time high and the school is calm, orderly, and importantly warm and welcoming for all; parents comment on how happy the school is.

The school now receives requests for visitors from other schools to look at behaviour, and this has been helped by previous external visitors to the school. Elliot is proud to show the school off, he has worked on the change. He asks visitors to select the classes they want to visit, and there are no rooms in the school he's not happy to take visitors. He often starts the tour in the toilets and changing rooms; they are clean and pleasant as any great school should be. Children's art works are on display – untouched and undamaged, it's cultural.

Figure 7.1 Legacy – Amara

> What is important to Marco is that the headteacher recognises his efforts, and at parents meeting she always acknowledges him – she looks out of the window at him as opposed to in the mirror taking the credit all to herself. They have discussed what Marco should do now, he has been approached to apply for headships at other schools, and he will leave a legacy behind but he will also be able to improve the lives of more children by becoming a head of another school in a disadvantaged area. But he also knows that headship is very different from deputy headship, he also has a young family, and his wife is a teacher.
>
> With this in mind, what purposeful steps can Elliot, Amara, and Marco take – and other leaders in similar positions – to leave a powerful legacy?

1. **Creating a culture that lasts**: we believe that culture is a living and breathing part of every school. This is because the people in the organisation *are* the culture. As a result it can shift, become stronger, mutate, and evolve on an almost daily basis.

   a. Define your school culture: what is it you want it to be? What does the school look like at its very best because this is the culture you want to capture and reinforce. A strong vision (as seen in Chapter 3) will help inform the culture of your school. The culture is the enactment of your vision.

   b. Artefacts: for a culture to survive in your absence, it is important to develop artefacts and policies that support and uphold the vision and culture. This could include agreed ways of working.

   c. It's the way we do things here: a legacy culture should be in place when leaders depart – it should survive without the leaders' physical presence. It's what informs day-to-day staff behaviour without ever being written down. It's not obvious when it's strong but it's glaringly obvious when it's challenged.

   d. Powerful messaging: the school's culture needs to be highly visible for it to become the lived experience for all stakeholders. This can be strengthened in schools via slogans/mottos/idioms displayed in corridors, and made visible during any student and parental engagement. When it becomes part of the fabric of the school – meaning it is seen and heard every single day – it continues to grow and becomes a reference point for conversations. It brings us back to the "why". This feeds into the way things are done.

   e. Recruitment: it is vital that new employees (including volunteers such as governors) understand the organisation and its culture at their first engagement with the school. This should be evident through all school communication – does your school promotional material all align with your vision, values, and ultimately your culture?

2. **Development plans**: establishing school improvement and development plans which actually help the school improve ensures the organisation is left in a better place. Creating a development plan is complex and nuanced:

    a. Involve all stakeholders: we believe that all stakeholders need investment in the development plan for it to be highly effective. If the preferred vision is created by all we have collective buy-in to its success.

    b. Communicate long-term vision: provide real clarity about what success will look and feel like; create the long-term vision of the future so compelling that all stakeholders aspire towards it – this vision should be so powerful that it could survive without you and any new leader can recognise its value.

    c. Check: leaders should ensure that – in order to move purposefully towards the compelling better vision for the future – frequent and regular checks are in place – and not bolted on to the end of the academic year. Evaluations should be low-stakes and continuous: *how will I know if this is successful? Is this working? How do I know? How could it be better?*

    d. Timescale: leaders should consider the length of the development plan. Improving schools is complex and arguably requires time – some development plans need to stretch over three or five years, or, in fact, have different layers with different timescales. This prevents leaders from straying from the global vision for improvement.

    e. Do you need a new development plan? New leaders might feel compelled to create a new development plan and to discard the existing one. We'd urge new leaders to reconsider this and have the courage to keep hold of a plan that feels right and is working.

3. **Cultivating the right environment where people can choose to perform at their optimal level**: the right culture should create the conditions where staff choose to be their most effective – and this is not about giving more or doing more. We believe that staff can be effective and mostly operate on autopilot. We need the conditions where staff choose to be highly effective because their contribution towards the school's success will be valued and recognised.

    a. Ensure that as you walk the corridors you recognise and acknowledge every member of staff. No matter what your leadership position is, your co-workers will be crucial to the school's success. Ensure as a bare minimum you see and speak to every member in your direct team.

    b. Recognise staff contributions. This could be via a conversation, a letter sent home, or a global thanks in the staffroom. Be aware that staff can often feel left out of global thanks in the staffroom; did you recognise all that happened at the school? That's difficult and certain areas will carry more value to you. Systemise your approach so that the thank yous are not lost during pinch points in the year.

    c. Always allow staff to feed into the success of the school – you don't need to align with their thoughts and agree with each proposal, but listen to and show that you value their thoughts. Staff will appreciate your time even if you don't move on their suggestions.

    d. Are there aspects of the community that staff can plug into to develop the school? Can you create a legacy link with local councils, parent groups, local businesses that can be fostered and developed for years to come? Can you create the freedom to encourage staff to explore these options?

    e. Embrace joy!

4. **Leadership development**: leaders must grow other leaders – especially if they wish to leave a legacy. This is about finding time and space in the school day to shift leaders from the day-to-day operational matters and into a strategic space where leaders can grow and learn.

    a. Know your staff: what is it the organisation needs to do to fulfil their ambitions? What leadership opportunities can we provide? We have experience with all staff, including early career teachers, gaining experience of leadership development.

    b. How do you create opportunities for leadership roles at the school in times of challenging budgets? Consider offering the opportunity to shadow a post holder or experience strategic leadership meetings with the expectation to contribute.

    c. How do you create the conditions for staff to develop areas without the fear of failure or criticism. Are you prepared for staff to fail and then support them to go again? Talk to your staff about the value of intelligent failure: *we know that learning and failing go hand in hand here"* and *"we value failure – because without it we can't get to innovation.* (Read more in **Trust – Embracing Failure.**)

    d. Leaders are readers: establish a culture that research on effective leadership is valued by regularly exposing your team to high-quality leadership texts. We think it's important that senior leaders are part of this work, even if it's led by other staff at the school.

    e. Succession planning: how do you ensure that the culture of the school continues when you depart? Have you identified key staff that align with the expected culture to enable continued development in-line with the plan? Growth from within can allow a culture to continue.

5. **Hope**: we need to develop organisational efficacy so that schools and the individuals within them believe better is possible.

   a. Ensure that success is celebrated as the development plan is enacted. Staff will have contributed to each milestone – show them you value their contribution by regularly offering specific praise.

   b. Keep referring back to the preferred future and what it will look like when we arrive. If we manifest the journey we will see the opportunities open to us, and ensure they are embraced.

   c. Leaders must remain positive at all times and carefully select the language they use. All leaders should have support networks for when times are challenging but staff need the security of their relentless optimism: *we're not there yet – but we can get there.*

   d. Messaging from leaders, especially senior leaders, can be vital to develop hope: it is too easy for a divide between senior leaders and staff to occur if the messaging is poor. All staff are important – it's not senior leaders who did or didn't do something; we do it all together. Leaders should use the pronouns "us" and "we".

   e. Grasping reality: leaders need to be aware of reality, and hope cannot be misguided. Leaders need to understand the ground truths of the organisation and ensure their development plans are effective. Hope without strategy will never get you where you wish to be.

References

Johnson, R. (2023) *Time to Think: The Things that Stop Us and How to Deal with Them.* John Catt.

Kerr, J. (2013) *Legacy: What the All Blacks Can Teach Us about the Business of Life.* Constable & Robinson Ltd.

Myatt, M. (2016) *Hopeful Schools: Building Humane Communities.* Mary Myatt Learning Limited.

Radcliffe, S. (2012) *Leadership Plain and Simple.* Pearson Education Limited.

SECTION 2
Torchlight behaviours

Now we consider the tools (or oil) leaders can deploy to best use domain-specific knowledge – the cogs in our leadership model. The cogs are necessary for anything else to work. Even the interlinking torchlight behaviours will fail if the cog is not sufficiently developed and continually moving; when the cog is motionless it will rust and erode. Willingham (2008) stated that secure knowledge within the specific domain is required in order to properly understand and solve problems. This chapter will provide you with possible tools to respond effectively to the problems.

We can't hope to develop all school leaders' domain-specific knowledge in this chapter of our book (as much as we'd like to). Instead, what we hope this section will do is give you the tools to effectively use your domain-specific knowledge (Figure 1).

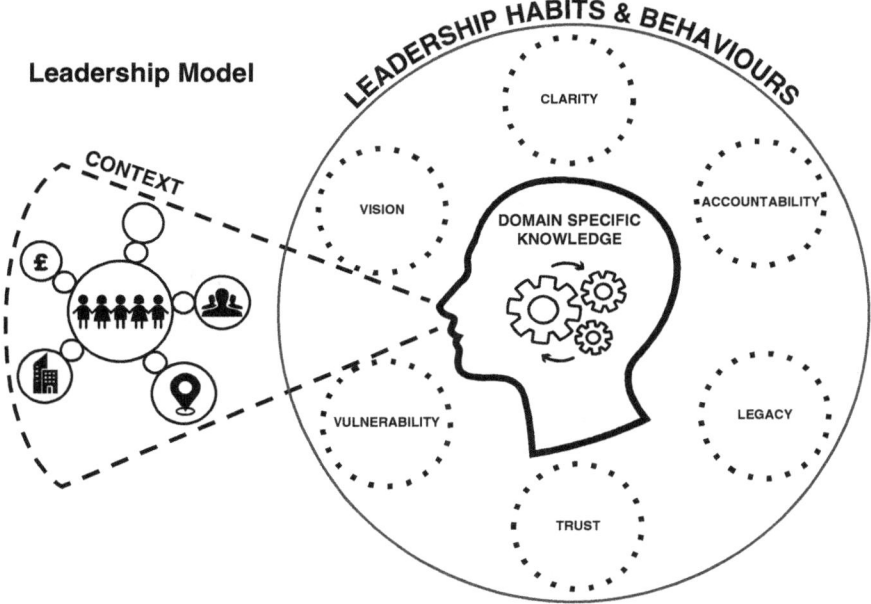

Figure 1 Leadership model

We believe that the way leaders think about the causes of the persistent problems they face influences their leadership practices. Causal reasoning is an essential cognitive competency for leaders – it enables us to predict future events and more effectively diagnose the problems we face in schools. We can better plan how to respond and which actions to adopt using cause-effect knowledge. Alongside Causal Reasoning, Situational Awareness – the ability to perceive and understand your environment, consider their meaning, and anticipate their future status – is what we believe makes you expert. Roger Kneebone (2020) says: "being expert is about how you think and see things", it is the "wisdom that allows you to get to the heart of a problem and fix it with skill, judgement and care". In other words, it gives you the power to flex your leadership – Kneebone calls this improvising – being able to respond to "the complex demands of a rapidly evolving situation".

This section of our book will provide you with the tools to perceive and understand your environment better and enable you to respond to the persistent problem with skill, judgement, and care.

References

Kneebone, R. (2020) *Expert: Understanding the Path to Mastery*. Penguin Randon House.
Willingham, Daniel T. (2008) Critical thinking: Why is it so hard to teach? Arts Education Policy Review, 109(4), 21–32.

8 Finding your voice

What is important?

We think the true significance of finding your voice as a school leader is highlighted when we consider a scenario where school leaders don't have a voice at work. Feeling like your voice isn't heard (or worse still, silenced) within your organisation or team is paralysing. And what is the cost of staying quiet (or silent) as opposed to speaking up? We have experience of senior leadership teams unable to challenge those above them in the organisation; every time this has weakened the capability and the decision-making of the senior leadership team.

In our experience, school leaders face two main challenges when they consider the voices within their organisation. First, to what extent leaders are confidently using their own voice. As Rachel Johnson in *Time to Think* (2023) explains, "as a leader, the team around you are looking for you to set the standards and expectations around the workplace culture". Being clear about your own ethos and values – and how to confidently and consistently signal these to those around us – is what will define the climate in your organisation. Second, as a school leader, the responsibility to ensure every individual voice in the organisation is heard, acknowledged, and valued becomes a key driver for the school's success and improvement. A leader who surrounds themselves – either consciously or subconsciously – with people that look and sound similar will not benefit from the power of diverse voices and perspectives. It is the school leader's responsibility to ensure voices are heard within the organisation for which they lead. We have written about how leaders can encourage other staff voices earlier in this book.

Having your voice heard at work contributes to both personal and organisational success. And we believe that finding, trusting, and using your voice aren't a constant or fixed state – rather, it is domain-specific and can shift and adjust.

Despite organisational and societal efforts towards greater diversity, leadership teams and roles can remain underrepresented. When you are sat at a table and you don't recognise any faces no one looks like you; no one sounds like you – it can feel beyond intimidating to find your voice and use it. To be clear, we don't think it is the responsibility of marginalised people to drive societal changes, or fix other people's biases in schools. We do, however, think that it is important to deliberately and purposefully get great at finding your voice, trusting your voice, and having your voice heard. When everyone feels able to express their opinions and perspectives, it promotes a culture of inclusivity and diversity. The more this is encouraged the more it becomes normal for all staff to be heard.

There are moments in school life when leaders use their voice routinely – in a way which feels automatic and reflexive, almost unthinking. In *Leaders with Substance*, Matthew Evans (2019) suggests that "mental scripts are habitual knowledge"; he compares this to not a literal script but rather your mind following a track, like a trail bike follows the well-worn tracks whilst out on a familiar ride. A Teaching and Learning Lead might have a strong mental script when discussing cognitive overload with a colleague – they can draw from a wealth of knowledge with ease and fluency. That same colleague may have to work more purposefully and deliberately – perhaps with a lack of fluency – when running their first reintegration meeting.

Interestingly, Evans goes on to consider the fact that "mental scripts become cultural scripts when they are followed most of the time by most of the people in the organisation". This can be a really powerful lever for school improvement at all levels – or an insidious degradation of standards. Cultural scripts determine, as Evans explores, "how things are done around here" – including how students behave during social time; how they move between lessons; how staff greet each other; who talks during staff meetings; whether the cups are left unwashed in the sink. As Evans says, "almost everything you can think of that happens in a school will follow a script. If only school leaders could influence cultural scripts, they would be the directors of the school's success".

Running parallel to this are the times in everyday school life that leaders need to find their voice in ways they might not have had to before – or, in fact, had the training to do so successfully. Leading your first meeting – the first time you chair a meeting – your voice needs to be clear and confident. Delivering to all staff or parents for the first time can be daunting – and at the same time is when you want your voice to be at its strongest. Leaders may also be using their voice to be an agent of change – to disrupt the status quo and create healthy agitation. Leaders might be using their voice to offer challenge and feedback in a way they've never done before. Perhaps leaders are running their first challenging absence meeting with a member of staff, or a meeting with an angry parent, and need to find a supportive, compassionate but clear voice. We have no doubt that the more a leader encounters these situations the more natural they become, and they create their own track that is increasingly clearer each time it is followed.

Finding your voice goes beyond the literal act of speaking and encompasses discovering and embracing your authentic self, values, opinions, and your unique way of expressing your thoughts and ideas – it is about having a deep understanding of your own identity as a leader and the desired identity of your organisation. School leaders can choose to script aspects of school life to influence the voice – and as a result, the culture of the organisation. An example of this might be scripting Line Management meetings – which ensures a consistent, ambitious voice is experienced by all.

School leaders need to get great at finding their voice – but within a leadership position in a school, it is also the leader's responsibility to help others find theirs. When individuals believe their contributions matter, they are more likely to be invested in their work and committed to the organisation's goals. Open communication channels facilitate better teamwork and collaboration – it is empowering. Employees who feel they can influence decisions or contribute to the school's direction are more likely to take ownership of their roles and responsibilities, leading to increased motivation and dedication. We think it is the leader's responsibility to create mechanisms to ensure every voice is heard.

Leaders can take purposeful and deliberate steps to ensure their team and organisation are rich with confident voices – including their own.

> **KEY TAKEAWAYS**
>
> - Leaders at all levels can take purposeful action to develop their own voice – and have a responsibility to develop others'.
> - Organisations and meetings free from conflict might be a symptom of staff feeling silenced.
> - Leaders can develop mental scripts to create a shortcut when responding to common problems – although there will be times when they are required to find their voice in a novel situation.

> Elliot decides to accept the position to become head of two schools. He understands that for this to be successful he must continue his drive to make great leaders at both schools. He will not be able to be at two places at once; he wants to help improve the new school whilst ensuring his current one continues to flourish.
>
> Elliot understands that developing other leaders is part of his responsibility. He wants his senior leaders to move into headship one day. To do this he wants to encourage them to share their voice and to hear their thoughts and ideas, some that might counter his ideas and that's fine (and indeed healthy). To do this he creates deliberate spaces to hear their voices. This is in senior leadership meetings, staff meetings and meetings with parents. Elliot ensures that he provides meaningful feedback to his senior leaders and they appreciate this as they know what he wants them to become, great leaders. Elliot also appreciates that just creating space to hear their voices is not enough. He has to develop their voices, but how?

Amara is now the line manager for two departments, English and technology. She has little knowledge of the technology department, or its staff, but is aware that the results are always the lowest in the school. Amara will often ask others to chair the department meetings, including the early career teachers; it's a good experience for them. She knows that often experienced leaders forget how big these things are for up-and-coming leaders. Her staff appreciate these opportunities and want feedback from her on how to improve. She often struggles to provide feedback, especially to the technology department. Some of this is due to her belief that she is not yet sure of what issues exist, but she has the backing of her headteacher to make the changes she needs. She needs to unpick the staff thoughts on where the department is.

Marco continues in his current role; he doesn't think all of his work on improving behaviour is embedded and cultural and wants to ensure it doesn't start to unpick for the children at the school. However, he is very aware that one day he will leave and he needs to develop other staff that work in his team to develop their skills. Marco routinely asks his pastoral staff to help him deliver presentations regarding behaviour to the local community (Figure 8.1). This can be quite challenging as not all the community are behind his drive to improve behaviour at the school. Some of his colleagues become nervous and worried about these presentations but want to support Marco. Marco finds presenting to large groups natural but he knows that at least one colleague needs his support. But what support can Marco offer?

With this in mind, what purposeful steps can Elliot, Amara, and Marco take – and other leaders in similar positions – to find their own voice? And help others find theirs?

Figure 8.1 Finding your voice – Marco

1. **Using your voice as a lever for change**: as a leader you have the potential to improve the lives of thousands of children. Your voice can be the lever for change for the community you serve and it's important that this flame remains burning within you and your team, even in the most challenging times.

   a. Why did you choose to work in schools? This is the origin of your voice. As a leader it's often not the voice that imparts knowledge to children; it's the voice that fights for your children to make their lives better. Align this passion with your leadership strengths to create change. At times recentre yourself with the origin of your voice, and it will provide you strength to continue to improve lives.

   b. What if you feel you are losing your voice? Whilst the pressure of academic outcomes and educational politics can distract you from your original voice it is always with you. Ensure you connect with people who share similar beliefs in education to enable you to continue to burn brightly. This could be in person or online.

   c. Give others a light: on your leadership journey there will be times when colleagues feel deflated and unable to make a difference. As a leader you can be the spark to rekindle their flame. Look for opportunities to talk to colleagues about why they chose to work in schools, and creating spaces for them to share their origin can be just what they need. Think of asking questions such as "What is the difference you wish to make to the children at our school" and "What is it that drives you to work at our school"; these questions can often lead to deep conversations that the fast pace of school life does not allow. As the German polymath Albert Schweitzer (1924) wrote, "Often, too, our own light goes out, and is rekindled by some experience we go through with a fellow-man. Thus we have each of us cause to think with deep gratitude of those who have lighted the flames within us".

   d. The origin of your voice might be enhanced on your journey: as you progress to leadership and your understanding of educational systems develops your voice might be enhanced from your knowledge. When you see children being failed by the system because of the way they talk or the family income they have, your fire can burn even brighter. Research the areas that interest you, and develop your knowledge by reading relevant texts to give your voice even more power at a local and national level.

   e. How do you share your voice? As a leader you have the responsibility to articulate your voice. Think how this can happen? Could you write an article for a national institute or create a social media profile and write a blog?

2. **Everyone has a voice**: as Coyle (2019) states, "successful groups use simple mechanisms that encourage, spotlight, and value full-group contribution".

Your colleagues will speak out when they feel trusted; when they can be vulnerable safely; and when they feel a sense of connectedness.

a. Purposefully watch group discussions and notice who isn't having their voice heard. Highlight or spotlight those who have contributed, and ask to hear the voices which have remained reluctant:

A and B, you've shared some really useful and valuable thoughts on X and Y, which will help us get to a better place. C, can you share what you are thinking?

b. Create the conditions for healthy agitation by asking:

"Can anyone push back on that?"

"I'd like to hear from someone who disagrees with idea X. Who disagrees?"

"What are we not doing well at the moment?"

"Who has a really strong opinion on this one?"

"I need you to poke some holes in X?"

"What are we pretending not to know?"

c. In meetings and in other conversations with the people you work with, avoid interrupting, and avoid trying to add value. Instead, ask for more:

"Can you say more about that?"

"What else are you thinking?"

"That's interesting...keep going"

"What else?"

d. Reward what you want repeated – highlight moments of vulnerability and how they are benefiting the group.

"A, thank you for making yourself vulnerable and sharing your thoughts on X – it will help us achieve Y and Z."

"A, thank you for sharing your thoughts on X – I know that might have felt quite tough and you demonstrated vulnerability in doing so."

e. Seek to understand, and ensure conversations are rich and useful whilst encouraging moments of vulnerability by asking:

"A, have we missed anything?"

"A, what are you seeing from your perspective?"

"What are you thinking about this decision/conversation?"

"How are you feeling about this decision/conversation?"

3. **Delivering to parents/assembly/CPD**: Caroline Goyder (2020) believes that our voices matter more now than ever – and that our voice is our "buried treasure" – buried deep in our torso. Goyder believes that "voice is the expression of your aliveness. But sometimes expressing that aliveness can make you feel vulnerable". The following steps will help you deliver well to all staff during CPD; to prospective parents at Open Evening; to your department in a team meeting – when it really matters, use your voice well.

   a. Plan and rehearse: Goyder believes that good thinking and good writing create good speaking. We author our authority. Plan your speech – and distil it to a key message. Goyder suggests filtering your ideas through your own mind before expressing them to others; the more you tend to your thinking the more you will communicate something worth listening to.

   b. Use your instrument: your voice is an instrument. You can use any instrument well with practice – this is the case for your voice.
   - Open your resonator with a big yawn or a laugh.
   - Learn how to breathe diaphragmatically.

   c. Fuel your tank:
   - Your in breath fills the tank – breathe in through the nose. We breathe in to gather our thoughts and refuel.
   - Your speech/out breath empties your fuel – speak out through the mouth.
   - The longer the sentence the deeper the in breath to refuel – if you want to say a long line you need time to refuel.
   - Breathe to feel excitement – hold your breath a little and you'll feel nervous. Purposefully and meaningfully, control your breathing.

   d. Tone, pause, pace:
   - Tone: aim to deliver to the back of the room – that will engage your diaphragm. A low tone is influential.
   - Pause: powerful speakers pause regularly and naturally – particularly at the end of thoughts.
   - Pace: research suggests that a rate of about 3.5 words per second. As you practise, consider Goldilocks: Too fast? Too slow? Just right!

e. Energy goes where attention flows: focus your attention on your presentation like a laser.

- Avoid your mobile phone and checking your emails. Your breathing becomes shallow when checking your phone – the opposite of what you want!
- Order the butterflies: it is normal to feel like you've got butterflies in your stomach – getting them to fly in formation is what counts in the moment.
- Stretch: your body needs to be physically warmed up to deliver well – get the blood flowing.

4. **Preparing for an online meeting**: since the Covid pandemic schools and those that support them hold more meetings online than ever before. Successful meetings and their outcomes are rarely due to chance. For the meeting to be successful, preparation is essential. We believe that confidence and active engagement are essential for your voice to be heard.

    a. Prepare and practise: before the meeting, review the agenda and practise what you want to say. Be clear about your key points and practise speaking confidently. Deliberate practice is a key feature of successful meetings, especially when you are new to leadership.

    b. Check your settings: prior to the meeting starting make sure that you have checked you can get access to the meeting and your microphone and camera are working. If possible join the meeting a few minutes early to check; you don't want to be the leader that joins and can't be seen or heard!

    c. Speak clearly and concisely: when you speak, articulate your words clearly. Avoid mumbling or speaking too fast. If needed, put a note on your keypad to remind you to slow down and speak clearly. Often in longer meetings or when speaking about an area you are invested in, your voice can accelerate.

    d. Be careful that one voice doesn't take over the meeting: it could be that you set a time for each point on the agenda as this can help focus participants' thoughts. At the start of the meeting make it clear that we want to hear all voices today. If one voice becomes dominant others will switch-off. Be prepared to ask inputs to be pithy. There will probably be occasions when you need to step in to open the floor to others.

    e. Engage actively: use the features such as "raise hand" emoji or use the chat box to allow all to participate. Make it clear to those in the meeting how questions and feedback should be given – during the discussion or at the end of the agenda point. Once you have set these parameters for the meeting ensure you hold on to this or those in the meeting will become frustrated.

5. **Finding your voice with angry parents**: one of the most challenging areas as a new leader is when you need to meet with angry parents. Often the anger has not been created by yourself but as a leader you will be called upon to calm troubled waters. A survey by Brown Jacobson (Spring 2024) that represented 1,800 schools found that there is "clear evidence that the number of complaints from parents/carers to schools and academy trusts continues to rise, with 65% of respondents reporting an increase in complaints during this academic year and 47% of those respondents stating that the number has substantially increased".

It can be easy to lose your voice during these conversations but if you approach the meeting with professionalism whilst maintaining a commitment to your own beliefs your voice will be heard.

   a. Where will you hold the meeting? We often meet an angry parent in the school reception area; clearly this is not suitable for this type of meeting. Many schools often have a small room available near reception; if possible use this. If this is already occupied or you feel you need a larger room near other adults plan this before arriving at reception.

   b. Think of your body position: where are you standing or sitting for the meeting? You shouldn't need to dominate the room. In our experience it is best to sit down for this type of meeting at a table.

   c. Listen actively: begin by listening to the parents' concerns. Let them express their feelings without interruption. The parent could be relaying what their child has told them and this might not necessarily be the whole truth but it's important to let them speak.

   d. Know your school policies: these are the times when all the works you have undertaken as leaders on your school policies pay dividends. Be prepared to explain the policies as needed and why your school has to follow them. You could direct the parent to the school's complaint policy for example.

   e. Propose solutions: often we will need to investigate an issue and return to the parent once this work has been undertaken. Agree the timelines for when this will happen and make sure you stick to them. Schools make mistakes and there are times when we need to say sorry, we are human after all.

   (We do not believe any staff member should be subject to any abuse from a parent or member of the public and there are times when you will need to stop a meeting if you, or a member of your staff, are being abused. We have experienced these times, and whilst challenging you will know when someone is overstepping the mark, e.g. overly aggressive/derogatory comments about sexuality).

References

Browne Jacobson (Spring 2024) "School leaders survey findings." https://www.brownejacobson.com/BrowneJacobson/media/Media/education/SLS-findings-Spring-2024.pdf.

Coyle, D. (2019) *The Culture Code*. Random House Publishing.

Evans, M. (2019) *Leaders with Substance. An Antidote to Leadership Genericism in Schools*. John Catt.

Goyder, C. (2020) *Find Your Voice*. Random House.

Johnson, R. (2023) *Time to Think: The Things that Stop Us and How to Deal with Them*. John Catt.

Schweitzer, A (1924) *Aus meiner Kindheit und Jugendzeit (Memoirs of Childhood and Youth)*. C. H. Beck.

Managing your team

What is important?

In *Botheredness*, Hywel Roberts (2023) explores the word "phronesis", explaining that the word is Ancient Greek for "practical wisdom". Roberts (2023) goes on to reveal that "in other spheres, it's simply "living well" and "knowing what you want and what you don't want". It could be classed as the know-how you collect as you get better at something. The knack. The toolkit". As school leaders, we become skilled as we grow our knowledge and experience – but this often means we have to step into situations blindly before we can get better at it. Roberts (2023) says "it's the knowing what to do or what to say when you don't know what to do or say. And that happens in our trade *a lot*". Due to the nature of schools being in situations that you have never encountered before is not unusual, and school leaders show great agility to hold conversations and make decisions around complex issues that are often first encountered problems.

When school leaders lead a team for the first time, the joy – and sometimes anguish – of working with complex, unpredictable, feeling, changeable humans becomes evident very quickly. To get great at managing a team, you need to manage a team. But, as Roberts (2023) suggests, you need to grow your wisdom; build your phronesis. We often suggest to new leaders, especially headteachers, to consider the position as a new apprenticeship; it can take time until you feel you have control of the academic year ahead.

Creating purposeful and meaningful habits and routines to ensure the episteme of your team is practised consistently means that, even on the darkest Monday in January, with multiple unplanned absences, a full moon, and an unexpected upset parent waiting for you in reception, your team knows "how it is done here". Roberts (2023) explains that episteme can be "learned and understood". This is an important part of managing a team. Alongside this, phronesis can be grown and nurtured.

Schools are teams within teams – as a result leaders often have to display agility with how these teams, and the individuals within them, are managed and led to obtain the best possible outcomes for the children. Leaders must display high levels of emotional intelligence to be able to adapt to the teams' needs. We do not believe that expecting all staff to adjust to a leader's personality is healthy.

In *Leaders Eat Last* Simon Sinek (2017) believes that "truly human leadership protects an organisation from the internal rivalries that can shatter a culture. When we have to protect ourselves from each other, the whole organisation suffers". Creating and maintaining standard operating procedures within teams create safety and the predictability humans need to feel secure. In "The Power of Predictability" (*Harvard Business Review*) authors Stevenson and Moldoveanu explore that predictability builds the trust "that allowed people to synchronize their actions in mutually productive ways". Managing school teams is about looking for the moments that can be made predictable – it goes back to the episteme: how things are done around here.

Matt Gavin in "Leadership vs. Management: What's the Difference?" (2019) offers three helpful distinctions between leadership and management, which are useful for school leaders:

1. Process vs vision
2. Organising vs aligning
3. Position vs quality

Managing your team as a school leader means: establishing processes and systems, which create predictability and organising resources and staffing to ensure synchronisation and efficiency. Management is about removing confusion, misdirection, and demotivation so that your team can move closer to a common vision and purpose on a regular, consistent, and recurring basis.

KEY TAKEAWAYS

- Working and managing teams is complex and challenging and can be, as a result, cognitively demanding.
- Leaders can create clear routines to establish "how we do things here", which creates safety and predictability.

During the first few weeks at his new school Elliot is surprised, and somewhat shocked, at the lack of clarity at the school. Whilst the children appear to have guidelines for how to behave and act at the school it is clear staff do not. Senior leadership meetings are loose both at the operational and strategic level and staff give him a variety of responses to the same question. He certainly doesn't feel a sense of "how things are done around here". Before he develops his team he has to develop a sense of how things are done at the school. He starts to codify expectations using his experience from his previous single school headship, how senior leader meetings are run, staff meeting expectations, how staff treat each other; the list appears endless (Figure 9.1). He doesn't remember having to do this at such a scale at his past school, but perhaps that is because he spent over ten years at the school modelling the behaviour expectations – many areas didn't need writing down at such a pace, and it was an established culture.

Amara feels as though the technology department is fragmented, the staff have groups within the group and some are clearly working against each other, and that's impacting on the children and their outcomes. Amara feels as though separate cultures have been allowed to develop. That might be because the head of department didn't want to challenge staff and as a result staff subcultures developed. The department had some well-established staff with deep roots at the school and the head of department was fairly inexperienced for a head of department. It is clear to her that certain staff feel they run the department, or perhaps the school, and want things to continue as they always have.

Marco continues to impress with his commitment to the school and its children, but it's clear that a portion of the community don't value his approach. One small section of parents is active on social media and serial complaints are sent to school regulators. Marco is having to deal with phone calls from authorities to explain and provide evidence to each complaint sent. It's new territory for him and he worries it is putting pressure on the head and the team he works with. It's also adding pressure to him as dealing with these external agencies is worrying. He wants to ensure that the staff team are still with him.

With this in mind, what purposeful steps can Elliot, Amara, and Marco take – and other leaders in similar positions – to effectively manage their teams?

Figure 9.1 Managing your team – Elliot

1. **Not all meetings with your team will be strategic and visionary**: Running an operational check-in meeting with your team can help keep everyone aligned and informed.

    a. Set a consistent time/day and location: choose a consistent day of the week – or specific time each day for the meeting. This consistency helps everyone plan their day and manage their workload, and ensures that the meeting becomes a habit.

    b. Agenda every meeting: plan a consistent agenda and highlight key events, updates, and any critical issues or information that need sharing and possibly discussion. Keep the agenda concise to avoid lengthy meetings. Consider, depending on the team you lead, some of the following: cover for the day, challenges from the day/week before, staffing, upcoming deadlines, etc.

    c. Individual updates: if appropriate, dedicate time for each member of your team to share their updates. Encourage brevity and focus on relevant information. This is an opportunity to discuss progress, challenges, and upcoming tasks in summary form.

    d. Problem-solving: use this time to address any roadblocks or challenges your team is currently facing. If someone needs assistance or faces obstacles, the team can consider solutions together. Keep the conversation constructive and solution-oriented.

    e. Actions and next steps: summarise action items and next steps. Assign responsibilities, set deadlines, and ensure everyone knows what they need to do before the next check-in. Document these tasks for reference.

2. **Navigating internal politics:** and handling gossip effectively are crucial skills for all leaders. Responding to internal conflict within a team involves a delicate balance of assertiveness, empathy, and strategic thinking. It can feel uncomfortable to manage, but left unattended can become insidiously toxic.

    a. Effective communication: be transparent about decisions, changes, and organisational goals. When your team understands the "why" behind decisions, they are less likely to engage in negative politics. Foster open communication across all levels of the organisation. Encourage respectful debate and allow employees to express their concerns without judgement in a safe and helpful place.

    b. Create a human map: beyond formal hierarchies and job titles, recognise who influences decisions; understand their motivations and alliances and build purposeful relationships with influential members of your team. These connections can help you navigate politics effectively.

c. Stay professional: avoid gossip and, at all times, refrain from discussing personal matters or spreading rumours. Focus on work-related conversations and demonstrate professionalism in your interactions. Others will follow suit if they see you maintaining high standards.

d. Build alliances: observe patterns by noticing who aligns with whom in your team. Identify potential allies who share your values and goals. Actively involve influential colleagues in projects. When you help them to gain a sense of ownership and to succeed, they may reciprocate.

e. Reframe internal politics: whilst maintaining professionalism, use informal conversations to gather insights; understand power dynamics and hidden agendas. Be prepared to adapt and influence rather than resisting politics, and adapt to them.

3. **Swift conflict resolution:** is important for any successful, healthy team. Managing conflict and mediating disputes will ultimately encourage open dialogue and create harmony and safety within your team. Your HR team might be able to offer specific guidance.

   a. Identification: first, identify the source of the conflict. Encourage opposing team members to express their perspectives calmly. Have each person involved write a simple statement of the issue during a meeting – whiteboards are good for this as they can be wiped clean after the meeting – which feels suitably symbolic.

   b. Response: allow each person involved to respond to the issue and the other side's position and invite opposing team members to engage in a respectful discussion.

   c. Resolution: analyse all the facts of the situation. Use a systematic decision-making process (see our decision-making steps) to work towards a solution that is acceptable and feasible for all team members.

   d. Enactment: put the agreed-upon solution into practice and monitor progress. This step allows for necessary adjustments as needed – and you can warmly hold staff to account to enact the agreed actions.

   e. Follow-up: periodically check in with the team to ensure that the resolution remains effective and address any emerging issues promptly.

4. **It is important that you manage your team with predictability:** so that staff feel safe. Predictability enhances productivity, morale, and overall team effectiveness, creating a healthier work environment.

   a. Do what you say you're going to do. If you arrange lesson visits, make sure they happen. If you arrange a meeting make sure it happens. Stick to your word rigidly so your team recognises your reliability.

b. Consider creating a specific calendar for the academic year for your team so that there are no surprises.

c. Stop starting, start finishing: combat task-switching by limiting the number of tasks your team are working on simultaneously. Focusing on fewer items at a time leads to faster delivery and improved quality.

d. Transparent collaboration: keep colleagues informed about progress, challenges, and changes. Open communication builds trust and reduces uncertainty.

e. Carefully, deliberately, and purposefully manage your emotions – your team needs a level leader. An emotionally literate leader is an emotionally predictable leader.

5. **Adaptive decision-making**: in educational leadership, both novice and experienced leaders frequently encounter novel situations that demand management without prior experience or knowledge. These uncharted moments require adaptive decision-making and action – often completed blindly. Research suggests that gut instincts or intuitions are not mere fanciful meaningless responses but rather the result of complex processing in the brain – we can use this to help us in blind situations.

    a. Predictive processing framework: the brain acts as a large predictive machine, constantly comparing incoming information and current experiences against stored knowledge and memories from previous encounters. Listen to your gut to predict what will happen next.

    b. Automatic and subconscious: intuitions occur when the brain detects alignment or discrepancy between its cognitive models (formed from past experiences) and the present context. This processing occurs before conscious awareness kicks in – so it'll start doing the heavy lifting for you even before you get there!

    c. Listen closely to, and notice your emotions – emotions serve as evaluations of recent experiences or thoughts, functioning as a type of information processing – they can help you to take the right action when you're unsure.

    d. Ask for help! When you experience a new situation you may need to ask for help – all great leaders do. Seek someone who may have more domain-specific knowledge or expertise and learn hungrily from them.

    e. Reflect and validate: after experiencing an unknown situation, take a moment to reflect. Purposefully build mental models so that when a similar situation occurs it feels less alien and more automatic.

References

Gavin, M. (31 October 2019) "Leadership vs. management: What's the difference? | HBS online." *Harvard Business School Online*, https://online.hbs.edu/blog/post/leadership-vs-management. Accessed 14 February 2024.

Roberts, H. (2023) *Botheredness.* Independent Thinking Press.

Sinek, S. (2017) *Leaders Eat Last: Why Some Teams Pull Together and Others Don't.* Portfolio Penguin.

Stevenson, H. and Moldoveanu, M. (1995) "The power of predictability." *Harvard Business Review*, https://hbr.org/1995/07/the-power-of-predictability. Accessed 25 February 2024.

10 Developing your team

What is important?

The quality of leadership is second only to the quality of Teaching and Learning in improving student outcomes (Robinson, 2011) – and even more so for students from poverty. Developing others, therefore, is more than ensuring that the individuals in your team are getting better – developing others is essential to lead a successful school. We think leaders can establish day-to-day routines and habits which will ensure the conditions are created for continual development and improvement – because better is possible. In *Building Culture* Lekha Sharma believes that creating a culture of continuous improvement implies "we're *all* learning *all* of the time" and that this "stamps out feelings of inadequacy, professional competition, and complacency". Sharma goes on to summarise that a culture of continuous improvement in schools means that "conversations around improvement are frequent, regular, and warmly welcomed". Ensure conversations around improvement are commonplace with your team and take deliberate and purposeful action. Sam Crome in *The Power of Teams* suggests that "whatever the team, learning should be part of its core remit". Our experience of leading schools tells us there are many missed opportunities to learn together and get better in team meetings every week – regardless of the team. Understanding the Continuing Professional Development (CPD) requirements of your team, adeptly facilitating CPD activities, and rigorously assessing the resultant impact are vital endeavours to foster an unwavering commitment to professional growth and learning within the team under your leadership. School leaders have an obligation to develop their co-workers; leaders should always be developing future leaders to enable the continuation and improvement of the school system.

We also understand from our experience of improving schools that professional learning is not limited to meeting time. Regular and robust feedback is essential to ensure we all get better.

Dan Heath, in his book *Upstream*, emphasises the significance of feedback loops in driving improvement. He underscores the importance of identifying and addressing root causes of problems rather than solely reacting to their immediate symptoms. By implementing effective feedback loops, schools can begin to proactively prevent issues from recurring, leading to sustainable and meaningful improvement. However, establishing feedback loops where there have been none takes careful and considered leadership. This feedback could happen after a presentation, a meeting with a parent, an interaction with a student – at any time improvement and better is possible. Failing to do this is denying that member of staff a development opportunity. Brene Brown says "what stands in the way becomes the way". Brown believes that there are several leadership behaviours and cultural issues that stand in our way of improving – one of these is choosing comfort over courage, and avoiding tough conversations – or honest and productive feedback. In *Upstream*, Dan Heath suggests that:

> feedback loops spur improvement. And when they're missing, they can be created. Improvement shouldn't require heroism. You shouldn't be able to escape or avoid improvement – by being surrounded by robust feedback loops – you can't help but get better.

We believe that once feedback loops are introduced they can quickly, if led appropriately, become the normal way of working. Staff recognise and feel the benefits and often actively encourage feedback loops.

In *The Right Kind of Wrong*, Dr Amy Edmondson reveals that humans are "saddled with a 'negativity bias'" explaining that we:

> take in "bad" information, including small mistakes and failures, more readily than "good" information… we remember the negative things that happen to us more vividly and for longer than we do the positive ones. We pay more attention to negative feedback than positive feedback…bad, simply put, is stronger than good.

This is important intelligence for school leaders to consider when considering how best to develop and improve their teams.

> **KEY TAKEAWAYS**
>
> - Effective leadership is key to better student outcomes, especially for those from poverty. Leaders should foster a culture of continuous learning.
> - Regular feedback and CPD activities are crucial for growth. Feedback loops help address root causes and drive sustainable improvement.
> - Leaders should be aware of the tendency to focus on negative feedback and work to create a culture that encourages constructive feedback for continuous improvement.

Elliot is clear that now staff at the school have clarity on their expectations he can begin to develop feedback loops at every level. Without clarity first being established he knows feedback would feel meaningless – if they don't understand what the expectations are at the school, how can they aim for it? At one of his early senior leadership meetings Elliot was surprised at the lack of challenge that existed around the table. It was as though no one could comment on each other's portfolio area for fear of upsetting the group. This was alien to Elliot and he started to openly promote healthy conflict. He knew that the group had trust in each other; they are a tight group, but this appeared to be focused on supporting each other in their personal life and friendships, not to improve the school.

From conversations with staff in the technology department (Figure 10.1) it was clear that lot of focus was being put on trying to convince Amara who the best (or what some considered the hardest working) staff are within the department. Conversations around children, their outcomes, or enjoyment of the department felt lacking. Department meetings felt like when Amara first started to work with the science team, but more fragmented. Some of the established members within the "team" had never been challenged; they sat in the same seats in the staffroom and mainly complained about other staff or children at the school. They had rolled out the same three lessons per year during the annual staff appraisal system (that Amara was glad had now been removed) and had done enough to just carry on. Amara was sure this was going to change for the children's benefit.

Marco was having very challenging meetings with several parents, often the same ones repeatedly. When he was absent from school the others in his team would try to cancel the meeting – they had become scared of the meetings and the abuse they may suffer. It

Figure 10.1 Developing your team – Amara

wasn't acceptable to Marco that the staff felt this way. The school was so much better and staff satisfaction in their jobs had rocketed with high levels of staff retention. His next challenge was to support these staff so that they could continue without him.

With this in mind, what purposeful steps can Elliot, Amara, and Marco take – and other leaders in similar positions – to develop their teams?

1. **As a school leader the pace of innovation has never been quicker**: Schools in many countries are using more evidence-based practice than ever before. There has been an increase in using research findings to improve school quality (Slavin, 2020). As a leader we can no longer rely on models we have always used if we are to reach our full potential. By committing to continual learning leaders can anticipate what might work best in school development. The only thing that isn't going to change in schools is change.

    a. School leaders are confronted by a multitude of demands and complex issues daily: and we understand these pressures but find the time to read a relevant book; you might only read one chapter a week but each page will help you to develop. Don't be shy in letting your colleagues know what you are reading, and this can set a culture of research at your school.

    b. Use social media: social media now allows us to easily connect with national and international educationalists. Often these can be short articles or tweets that develop our knowledge. You often don't need to use your name to keep anonymity.

    c. Follow online sites: there are many excellent online websites that provide a wealth of knowledge for leaders. Find the ones most useful to you and create a link on your mobile phone so you can quickly jump onto the site when time allows. Often whilst waiting for a partner or for the children to finish an after-school activity you can jump on for a quick catch-up.

    d. Sign up for blogs: subscribe to daily or weekly blogs. It wasn't that long ago when leaders had to pay for subscriptions for useful daily blogs. Today you can pick the ones best suited for you. Whether that be in curriculum design, teaching and learning, pastoral or retention strategies – the list is endless! Often at the start of each day you can quickly read the latest areas of interest over your morning drink of choice.

    e. Engage with professional development opportunities. Whilst school budgets are restricted, it is important that leaders have the opportunity to develop themselves as well as their staff. Undertake high-quality professional development, perhaps one recommended by a colleague or mentor. Research the one you commit to, and make sure it's of value and worthy of your time.

2. **Leaders set the tone for the school**: schools need to be engaged with research and developing new learning. This culture needs to be developed by the leaders at the school. In some schools you witness small groups of staff that engage, or even on an individual level, but unless it's the culture of the school – it's what we do around here, you will hinder developing the school's full potential (and learning won't be connected but disjointed).

    a. New learning is what we do as leaders: at each senior leadership meeting allow time to discuss some pre-reading that has been shared with the team at least 48 hours prior (even better if it's a chapter of a book each week so leaders can choose the time to read that best suits them).

    b. How can new learning improve the school development areas? Ensure that when discussing the development areas for the school the suggestions for improvement are based on research not simply on gut feelings (as useful as these can be).

    c. When staff ask questions: think of the learning you have undertaken and share this with colleagues who ask relevant questions. They will understand that you are a leader who reads (leaders are readers!). You will also be able to share learning with each other so you both develop.

    d. Create a reading library: find a space in the staffroom or online to recommend good books recently read by staff and what areas of school improvement they helped with.

    e. Everyone is a leader: in many schools we have experienced it feels as though only leaders can be engaged with leadership development. Offer a short leadership development opportunity for all staff on a weekly basis (ensure you don't cancel one or staff will stop attending as they build their busy life around prior commitments). This is not only a great way for staff to see their leaders engaged with research but it also develops future leaders at the school (all staff are leaders!).

3. **Create a school that is a research-based institute for all its staff**: To solve the issues we are dealing with, or will deal with, at schools we often require new knowledge. It is through the investment in developing our staff that success will occur, and this learning needs to be consistent.

    a. Create a space for learning to occur: we cannot simply tell our staff to research and hope that it will happen. Calendarise the time before the academic year commences where learning will occur.

    b. Plan the content: what is it our co-workers need to know and are you sure? Think about early career teachers, heads of department, pastoral leaders, and senior and executive leaders. What learning is best for them and how does this fit with the school improvement priorities?

c. How will this new knowledge be delivered? Pre-think how you want the new knowledge to be delivered. Don't leave this until the day before; the time is too important. Is it all the staff together, break out rooms, online, pre-reading or all of these?

d. Can you link with other schools or educational establishments? Could it be that you can share your proposed learning with other local schools and share resources? Staff could join remotely or have face-to-face termly meetings. This allows colleagues who are often isolated to join others with similar portfolio areas.

e. How do you know it's been effective? If your staff have committed to the new learning, how do you know that it's been effective and is there learning to do to make it even better next time? Don't lose the opportunity to grab real feedback (anonymous is better).

4. **Feedback loops can drive improvement**: These loops can prevent issues from reoccurring as feedback can be given; not to do so simply denies a co-worker a learning opportunity.

a. A feedback loop provided to a colleague is a gift of improvement: in many schools feedback loops are still unusual and it needs to be implemented thoughtfully. In our experience it is often useful for leaders to start to ask for feedback after an activity such as a school assembly. Ask a colleague to provide feedback on how the assembly could have been improved – this can break down the feeling of its leaders "doing it to us". As leaders we want to improve so grab as many opportunities for feedback as possible. Make it normal practice.

b. Think of who you choose for your feedback loop: of course ask a trusted colleague at first but then think of others you could ask. We have asked teaching assistants, administration staff, and early career teachers for feedback – they will provide useful feedback that your closest colleagues might not see.

c. It can be the small things: a feedback loop does not only have to be after a whole staff meeting or large presentation. If you have a colleague with you after you have spoken with a member of staff or child ask how that went and what you could have done to improve.

d. Courage over comfort: it is very comfortable not to provide feedback or simply tell a colleague what it is you think they want to hear, but we don't improve by being told it's all perfect (and it probably isn't in our feedback experience!). Create a culture of continual improvement for all.

e. Think about when you employ new colleagues: in an interview explain to potential new colleagues that the school uses feedback loops to improve us all. This way they can decide if a school driving for improvement is for them and also if appointed they will expect to receive feedback – it won't be a surprise to them.

5. **Stand on the balcony**: Catch your staff being good and share this with colleagues. As leaders we have to be careful not to get lost in what it is we are doing and not seeing our colleagues and the great work they are doing. When you spot this, ensure you catch it and allow others to learn from it.

   a. Schools have great collective intelligence: but how often do you witness a colleague doing great work and it's not shared due to the hustle and bustle of everyday school life. Find a space for colleagues to share this work with the whole team – you could use a morning briefing for example.

   b. Use technology to capture moments: if you witness a colleague with a strength, such as the use of questioning, video the session and create a school library of these moments to allow others to learn from someone in your school with your children – it can be much more powerful than a clip from a school you can't relate with.

   c. If you lead a team how can you share moments? If you lead a pastoral team for example and witness a colleague successfully supporting a dysregulated child. It could be that at the next pastoral meeting you role-play what happened and break down why your colleagues took certain actions and how that helped calm the incident.

   d. How do you share professional learning from outside the school? We have experienced applying for professional development outside of our school context and been asked to present on what we learnt only for this never to happen, and our colleagues would often say the same (often it just felt like a box to tick on the application form). Again, pre-plan the year ahead, and find the space to share learning, be this live or in a school resource bank – don't let this new knowledge disappear or be stuck on location.

   e. Celebrate colleagues and the new learning they are undertaking: often schools have staff at all levels developing themselves via lengthy professional development. We often hear of staff within schools undertaking master's degrees and have inquired around the topic areas. The responses we have had included the use of performance targets for staff, the use of topic booklets to improve learning, and lots more. Asking these staff to share their new knowledge with colleagues can lead to small groups of staff working together on projects that can quickly become whole school drives for improvement.

References

Brown, B. (2019) *Dare to Lead*. Random House Publishing.

Crome, S. (2023) *The Power of Teams: How to Create and Lead Thriving School Teams*. John Catt from Hodder Education.

Edmondson, A. (2023) *The Right Kind of Wrong: Why Learning to Fail Can Teach Us to Thrive*. Penguin Random House.

Heath, D. (2020) *Upstream*. Bantam Press.

Robinson, V. (2011) *Student-Centered Leadership*. Jossey-Bass Leadership Library in Education.

Sharma, L. (2023) *Building Culture. A Handbook to Harnessing Human Nature to Create Strong School Teams*. John Catt Educational Ltd.

Slavin, R. E. (2020) How evidence-based reform will transform research and practice in education. *Educational Psychologist*, 55(1), 21–31. https://doi.org/10.1080/00461520.2019.1611432. Accessed 10 August 2024.

 Managing change

What is important?

Matthew Evans (2023), in his blog "The 7 inconvenient truths of school improvement planning", reminds his readers that:

> not everything needs to improve all of the time. If we are too busy improving things, we'll forget to cherish what we have. And the inconvenient truth is that we can only work at improving a fraction of the things we'd really like to improve at a time.

Understanding that our capacity to devote the time and energy that change demands in order to be effective is limited, creating systems and mechanisms to identify the right thing to improve at the right time is fundamental to any effective change in schools. Vivian Robinson's *Reduce Change to Increase Improvement* (2017) suggests that school leaders should be motivated by a "dissatisfaction with the status quo and a determination to reach something better". Robinson explains that "the belief that change is possible motivates the effort required for improvement". In our experience, school leaders should remain outward-facing to ensure their vision of better shifts and grows – and isn't static or unmoving. A resistance to change in school teams, a defensiveness which stunts growth, and an approach that favours comfort (and clinging onto the status quo) over growth should be recognised and responded to by school leaders. Robinson goes on to question how leaders "communicate their dissatisfaction… in a way that is uplifting rather than demoralising" in order to change human behaviour – which is the fifth inconvenient truth that Matthew Evans writes about. Evans believes that "it is much harder to change how people behave than we would like to admit" and that staff must be provided with a compelling reason why they should "adapt their daily actions" in order for the change to succeed. Robinson suggests that one strategy to do this is to adopt an engagement model – as opposed to the bypass approach. Robinson's engagement model seeks to explore and understand the beliefs that sustain the current practice school leaders may wish to change. The bypass model is often employed in situations where there is resistance to change or when existing systems are perceived as ineffective or hindering progress – but often the beliefs that are sustaining the current practice aren't altered.

Robinson emphasises the importance of "problem talk" in her work. She suggests that effective school leaders engage in constructive dialogue around identifying and addressing challenges within their settings. Problem talk openly acknowledges problems, discusses their underlying causes, and collaboratively generates solutions. Robinson argues that problem talk fosters a culture of transparency, trust, and continuous improvement within schools, ultimately leading to more effective leadership and change practices and ultimately, better outcomes for students.

In our experience of leading change in school, John Kotter's seminal framework for change management has been an effective and successful tool to use. Beginning with establishing a sense of urgency, leaders create momentum by communicating the need for change and rallying stakeholders around a shared vision. Through building a powerful coalition and articulating a clear vision, leaders inspire commitment and alignment across the organisation. Effective communication ensures that the vision is understood and embraced by all, while empowerment facilitates broad-based action and innovation – leaders empower their staff to take ownership of the change process by removing obstacles, providing resources, and fostering a culture of innovation, experimentation, and continuous improvement. Celebrating short-term wins sustains momentum and credibility, paving the way for further progress. Consolidating gains and anchoring new approaches in the school culture strengthen the changes, ensuring their long-term sustainability. It is our experience that, by following Kotter's eight steps, leaders can navigate the complexities of change management with clarity, purpose, and effectiveness, ultimately driving positive change and improvement.

Managing change of course leads to questions about the school's improvement plan. In our experience these can be overly lengthy, often ignored by senior leaders once written and produced to keep external auditors or boards of school happy – it becomes a compliance exercise. In other schools the development plan links directly to cycles of inquiry alongside their timelines. The plan is visible in school offices, timelines pinned to walls and checked at senior leadership meetings for impact. Timelines can vary in length depending on the development area and allow flex – schools need to be agile. Sometimes the most successful improvement plans are those when leaders have really considered capacity for change before writing the document.

We also believe that improvement plans should be in place at the start of the academic year. Too often we witness them being written after the first term commences. Schools will already have knowledge of what it is they need to improve and their expected results at the end of the previous academic year. They might need tweaking slightly post results but time prior to the start of a busy new year is time well spent.

> **KEY TAKEAWAYS**
>
> - There is a difference between change and improvement. Leaders should guard against change that doesn't lead to improvement.
> - Changing human behaviour is complex and hugely challenging – if leaders don't engage with the beliefs that are sustaining the practice they want to chance, then change becomes even harder to navigate.
> - Leaders can lean on an existing model for change to ensure they have an appropriate tool to guide and make change stick.

Elliot has spent time developing the vision for the future in his new school. The staff appear keen to improve; they don't enjoy being the school that is the parents' "second choice". Through conversations he understands that the school has been through change after change. It's like a Christmas tree school – one light flashes and they chase that and then they shift to the next bright light; nothing ever lasts. Previous leadership appears to have added initiative after initiative; whatever was on social media that weekend would be enacted on a Monday.

Elliot explains that he wants to focus on world-class basics, nothing new will be added after the school improvement plan has been agreed. Elliot also wants all staff to be involved in the development plan, collective intelligence and buy-in is important to him. He knows if staff have an input it's easier for them to see the vision. Elliot has high aspirations for the school, and he is determined to succeed for the children.

The departments Amara line manages are now more together; she knows this is because she has codified actions within the department. Meetings, behaviour, teaching and learning, marking, assessment, and resources all have clarity. She has removed the ambiguity that often caused confusion and conflict. Amara knows that the departments have different staff with different personalities and she manages them with this knowledge, and it's not one-size-fits-all.

Amara is really pleased that in department meetings now a healthy challenge exists; this is built on the trust that she has built since becoming line manager. Historically this would have caused upset and fall outs; now it's expected. The departments would rather speak openly and discuss each other's work as that is what's best for the children, and it's not about putting staff feelings ahead of what's right. This feels light years away from her starting point.

Marco stays true to what's right for the school; he doesn't shift and bend to the parent pressure being put on the school. The children are thriving and performing better than ever, and they are also happier as are the staff (Figure 11.1). He can keep the school staff together because he has created a crystal clear vision for what behaviour could be (and it's getting closer each day). The whole school is tight and committed because they can feel the benefits. Marco continues to overcommunicate the vision; ask any staff member and the clarity is obvious.

That said, Marco is happy to adjust and tinker with behaviour, and until leaders act it's not always possible to see all the potential outcomes, he is fine-tuning and communicating.

With this in mind, what purposeful steps can Elliot, Amara, and Marco take – and other leaders in similar positions – to manage change?

Figure 11.1 Managing change – Marco

1. **Prioritising change**: school leaders require discernment in navigating through a multitude of change priorities, recognising that not all changes can be implemented simultaneously. Often, the school's immediate context and need influence the urgency and extent of change necessary. In instances where a school is safe and excelling, a measured and deliberate approach – "hurrying slowly" – is prudent. Conversely, in situations where a school is grappling with safety concerns and poor teaching, swift action is imperative. It is crucial for school leaders to judiciously prioritise changes, ensuring that each step taken aligns with the institution's immediate needs and long-term goals.

    a. Prioritise safeguarding: the first step for any leader is to ensure the safety of the students and staff. No other step is more important. Conduct a safeguarding audit and act on any findings.

    b. Using the Value Complexity Matrix determine what constitutes "value" and "complexity" for your school or project. Value could be measured in terms of impact on student outcomes or strategic alignment. Complexity might include technical difficulty, resource requirements, or time constraints.

c. Evaluate each possible priority against the established criteria. Rate them on a scale (e.g. 1–5) for both value and complexity. This will help in comparing priorities relative to each other.

d. Plot on the quadrant: create a two-dimensional chart with "value" on the y-axis and "complexity" on the x-axis. Plot each priority on the chart based on their ratings. This visual representation will help you see which priorities fall into the categories of Quick Wins, Big Bets, Maybes, or Time Sinks.

e. Now prioritise accordingly: use the quadrant to make informed decisions. Typically, you'd prioritise "Quick Wins" first as they provide significant value for relatively little complexity. "Big Bets" might require more planning and resources but can also be crucial for long-term success. "Maybes" can be considered if there's extra capacity, while "Time Sinks" are usually avoided.

2. **Understanding change is important** – and really understanding it is any leader's first step to ensure the problem has been seen and is being addressed – rather than the symptom the real problem is creating. You can't begin to prepare your team – or the school – for change until you can clearly define it with clarity and precision.

    a. Define the "Why": start by articulating the rationale behind the change: what is prompting the change? What makes it essential at this moment? How is the current situation unsatisfactory, and what improvements are expected?

    b. Identify symptoms and desired outcomes: recognise the signs that indicate a need for change. Which symptoms of the problem are most visible? Envision how these symptoms will be alleviated or transformed once the change is implemented.

    c. Evidence-based approach: protect against biases by systematically gathering data. Collect evidence from various sources to substantiate the need for change. Use triangulation to cross-verify information and ensure a comprehensive view.

    d. Pros and cons assessment: evaluate the change's worthiness. Quickly list the benefits and drawbacks. Determine if the anticipated outcomes justify the required resources and effort.

    e. Communicate clearly: detail the practical implications of the change. How will the change manifest in everyday activities and behaviours? Ensure that the proposed change is supported by evidence and clearly understood by all stakeholders.

3. **Using a model for change**: leaders at all levels can use Kotter's model for change to ensure they take deliberate and purposeful action towards successful improvement.

   a. Create a sense of urgency: inspire action by emphasising the need for change and the opportunity it presents by highlighting the risks of maintaining the status quo and the benefits of change.

   b. Build a guiding coalition: form a committed team to guide and coordinate the change effort by identifying influential and diverse leaders across the school that will bring different perspectives and represent the organisation.

   c. Develop a strategic vision: clearly articulate the desired future state and gain buy-in by clearly communicating the why and what of change.

   d. Empower action: remove barriers and empower employees to take part in the change process by looking for physical obstacles – as well as speaking to your team's fears.

   e. Generate short-term wins: celebrate early successes to maintain momentum and engagement.

4. **Involving staff**: the Educational Endowment Foundation (EEF) states that "people, ultimately, value what they feel part of". Involving staff, students and the wider community in change and implementation will determine the success of the change. The EEF suggests that leaders should "engage people so they can shape what happens while also providing overall direction".

   a. Once you know and understand the change, you should aim to engage the people you lead early on, so that they can meaningfully input into the proposed change. If active engagement is the aim, consider preparing a short document or recorded message which provides an outline of the proposed change so that when you meet with staff, they have had time to consider their perspective, generate ideas, and consider concerns.

   b. When you meet with staff, consider using hedging language so that staff know it is not already set in stone!

      - Modal verbs: could, may, might
      - Adjectives: possible, probable, likely, unlikely
      - Adverbs: conceivably, perhaps, possibly

   c. Create a safe and purposeful arena for the wider school community to engage. If appropriate, consider how to engage hard-to-reach families.

   d. Once the people you lead and the community have had the opportunity to influence change, create space for collaboration. Consider creating a working party or an implementation team.

e. Regular communication throughout the implementation can help to ensure active engagement throughout the process. Consider how best to share progress and successes with the people you lead.

5. **Fast or slow?** As explored in Step 1, there are times leaders will need to implement change swiftly, and other times they can "hurry-slowly". Robinson highlights the importance of engaging with your colleagues' beliefs – rather than bypassing them – in order to create sustainable change. Sometimes slowing down is a way of speeding up.

   a. Identify existing beliefs: understand the preconceived beliefs and assumptions held by teachers and other staff. Engage in dialogue to uncover these underlying mental models.

   b. Challenge assumptions: encourage teachers and other staff to critically examine their beliefs. Discuss how these assumptions might impact their practice and limit improvement.

   c. Modify beliefs: facilitate a shift in staff thinking. Provide evidence, experiences, and alternative perspectives to modify existing beliefs.

   d. Align practices with new beliefs: help teachers align their instructional practices with the revised beliefs. Support them in implementing strategies consistent with the desired changes.

   e. Monitor progress: continuously assess the impact of the modified beliefs on teaching practices and student outcomes. Adjust as needed.

References

EEF. Education Endowment Foundation (24 April 2024) "A school's guide to implementation." https://educationendowmentfoundation.org.uk/education-evidence/guidance-reports/implementation. Accessed 7 July 2024.

Evans, M. (2023) "The 7 inconvenient truths of school improvement planning." https://educontrarianblog.com/2023/05/28/the-7-inconvenient-truths-of-school-improvement-planning/. Accessed 3 March 2024.

Kotter, J. "The 8-step process for leading change | Dr. John Kotter." *Kotter International*, https://www.kotterinc.com/methodology/8-steps/. Accessed 7 July 2024.

Robinson, V. (2017) *Reduce Change to Increase Improvement*. SAGE Publications.

Sharples, J., Eaton, J. and Boughelaf, J. (2024) *A school's guide to implementation*. Education Endowment Foundation.

12 Leading Quality Assurance

What is important?

We believe there is a place for Quality Assurance in schools – but that Quality Assurance should do two things: (1) it should be focused on systems and processes – not people and (2) it should always feed into improvements: it should make things better.

Regardless of the leadership position held in schools, "the more leaders focus their relationships, their work, and their learning on the core business of teaching and learning, the greater their influence on student outcomes" (Robinson, 2011). Interestingly, leadership in "higher-performing schools…is much more focused on the business of improving learning and teaching" (Robinson, 2011). We cannot hope to understand what is happening in classrooms unless, as leaders, we spend time in classrooms in our schools. "Leaders influence students indirectly by creating the conditions required for teaching and learning" (Robinson, 2011) – but we can't evaluate whether we have established the right conditions – and the right systems to support our teachers – unless we are Quality Assuring them.

It can be a difficult challenge for leaders to get the quality assurance balance right. We have experience of visiting schools and speaking with staff who are frustrated at the amount of lesson drop-ins that occur. In one school staff spoke of times when four adults would arrive to quality assure their lesson. This amount of adults can, of course, cause attention issues for students and four staff to observe the same 15 minutes of a lesson appears unusual, and not entirely healthy. At the other end of the spectrum staff have spoken with us who rarely receive a lesson visit. At this end of the spectrum, staff can become frustrated that apparently no one cares about the good work that they are doing each day. We believe these two ends of the spectrum are not helpful – one is possibly evidence of staff losing autonomy and feeling permanently under the microscope – the other not having any quality assurance to speak of so how leaders know how good their systems and processes are at their school is difficult to fathom.

In *Reduce Change to Increase Improvements* (2011), Robinson states that "change is an extremely disruptive and costly process, in both a material and psychological sense". Whether the change is a new curriculum, a Teaching and Learning rubric, or a new behaviour system, the product or system needs to be Quality Assured to check it is having the desired outcome. When leaders plan and manage change carefully – purposefully avoiding changing too much and not improving anything – they must ensure the change they've carefully implemented is doing what it was intended to do – and that it continues to do so.

We believe the best school leaders spend time in the classrooms in their schools. Not only is it a necessary and important responsibility for all school leaders, it is where the magic happens; it is a joy to spend time where teaching and learning is happening.

In today's climate of teacher shortages we believe that quality assurance leads to improvements across a school. This could be assuring how effective staff coaching is at a school or a recent professional development opportunity and viewing its impact in the classroom. We often talk of loving the ones you have and shining each member of staff to be the brightest diamond they can be – because we can all get better. The idea that senior leaders can replace staff with "better" ones is simply untrue. We have personally witnessed many staff that have "moved on" from a school only to flourish in another with the correct culture. We have little doubt that the recruitment crisis and numbers of teachers leaving the profession early will only lead to a need for greater quality assurance and staff development – not less.

In *Intelligent Accountability* (2020) Didau offers two models of school leadership: the deficit model and the surplus model. Didau explains that "in a surplus model, because no one is "to blame", the psychological safety exists to focus on identifying and eliminating the reasons for problems so they don't reoccur". The deficit model does the opposite – often placing blame at teachers' feet. Interestingly, Didau suggests that "one of the most bitter ironies is that schools who most need to operate a surplus model – schools considered to be failing – are also those where the risk of doing so may seem untenable". We think it is important to view Quality Assurance through a surplus model of school leadership. As Quality Assurance in schools is evaluating systems and processes – and not people – when problems are brought to light, leaders must adopt a problem-solving mindset.

We're aware that Quality Assurance often brings with it negative connotations – sitting alongside a lack of autonomy and top-down control and power. We don't believe Quality Assurance needs to be led or conducted in this way. We believe effective Quality Assurance can actually not only help leaders effectively measure the impact of a system or process – it can also bring about improvements. Quality Assurance in classrooms can highlight further professional development needs and can reveal the student experience to leaders in an authentic way.

The Education Endowment Foundation (EEF) recognises the value of uniting implementation processes suggesting that "uniting extends to the values and practices that relate to the process of implementation itself" including "developing a shared belief that monitoring implementation is key to enabling ongoing improvement, rather than playing a punitive accountability function, can fundamentally change how staff feel about implementation".

> **KEY TAKEAWAYS**
>
> - Quality Assurance does not need to be synonymous with punitive accountability.
> - Done right, Quality Assurance can support school improvement.
> - Leaders should focus on Quality Assuring processes and systems, rather than people.

Elliot has the plans and strategy for school improvement agreed. All the staff have contributed to the development plan. He knows too much change will not help, so they focus on what will make the biggest difference. Elliot also knows that he must have effective quality assurance in place for the development areas. Some areas will need a greater focus, some involve all staff, some just a few, but all are important to the success of the school.

Elliot ensures that all areas have effective timelines and spaces to quality assure their development. He doesn't want them to be forgotten or ignored for months. Some will need tweaking as they progress, some need major change, and most are successful. Elliot has ensured that each adjustment is based on evidence to increase the chances of success (Figure 12.1).

Amara has the two departments she manages working effectively. The two teams trust each other and now she must focus on improving the outcomes for the children. Amara understands that until she built trust in the team, developments would have proven difficult, if not impossible. Her focus is on improving the teaching and learning in the departments, especially in her new department, technology. The historical issues of how you can't apply pedagogical practice into technology have gone and the staff have a real focus and drive to improve. Whilst she leads the process the department collectively designs their improvement plan. They agree that all staff should be part of quality assurance of the teaching within the department; they have set time to visit each other's classes, allocate a trusted responsive coach to the team, and ensure that they work to develop not simply judge lessons. The quality of teaching is discussed at each department meeting. Amara knows that the quality of teaching is her most important gift to the children and the department knows that unless they have rigorous quality assurance how will they know it's making a difference.

Marco needs to ensure that the behaviour refinements he is making are proving effective at the school. He can't afford to wait long periods of time without checking in on its progress. He regularly takes staff, pupil, and community voice. He compares the outcomes with previous points in time and looks for changes. Marco shares this with senior leaders and staff at the school, and he believes that it is no use collecting information and then not sharing the outcomes with the staff – without their input he has

Figure 12.1 Leading Quality Assurance – Elliot

no reference point. He remembers completing quality assurance questionnaires only for them never to be spoken about again, he lost trust with them.

With this in mind, what purposeful steps can Elliot, Amara, and Marco take – and other leaders in similar positions – to lead Quality Assurance?

1. **Culture**: for Quality Assurance to be meaningful – for it to provide you with an accurate and useful snapshot of the system/process you need to check – the culture needs to be right. If you're introducing Quality Assurance in a school where there hasn't been any – or perhaps the type of Quality Assurance that has come before you has felt punitive and focused on people – it is important you purposefully work to ensure the culture is right.

    a. Sell the why to your senior leadership team – ensure there is understanding within your school leadership team. Talk to your senior leadership team about previous Quality Assurance at the school – and what impact this had on the culture: do staff fear it? Is there an open-door culture?

    b. Visiting other school settings is useful to scrutinise how other leaders best use Quality Assurance. Ensure you are outward-facing and look for good practice outside of your own context.

    c. Sell the why to your staff. You'll want to communicate the purpose of the Quality Assurance deliberately – planning and rehearsing your message are really important, particularly if you're beginning a shift in culture.

d. Create a system for Quality Assurance that works and is predictable. Consider how much time you (and others) can realistically give to Quality Assurance each week – and create an efficient and useful method of collecting the information gained during Quality Assurance.

e. If members of your team are tasked with Quality Assurance then hold them warmly to account (you can refer to the steps on **Accountability** to help you).

2. **Understanding Quality Assurance**: to lead effective Quality Assurance, you need to interrogate what it is you have chosen to Quality Assure and why this, why now?

    a. Identify what to Quality Assure: focus on systems and/or processes that have the highest impact – and know your why: why and how will Quality Assuring this area lead to improvements?

    b. Understand the system/process: you need a clear idea of what the active ingredients are of the area you'd like to Quality Assure – this should, where appropriate, be evidence-informed.

    c. Communicate with staff – including the union representative in your school. Now ensure your team has a clear idea of the active ingredients – this doesn't mean there isn't room for adaptations and mutations (not all mutations are lethal!). Give your staff time to practise and rehearse where necessary.

    d. Communicate a timescale: how long will you be Quality Assuring this area for? A week? A half-term? An academic year? Be sure you're clear what Quality Assuring this area over time will give you.

    e. Commit to it: once you've planned the area to Quality Assure, and communicated with your staff, do it. There will always be competing demands on your time – prioritise this so that your staff know you'll do what you say you're going to do.

3. **Celebration**: ensure that Quality Assurance leads to meaningful celebration of what's going well. Quality Assurance should not be happening in secret – it should be transparent and completely unambiguous.

    a. When you have clarity about the active ingredients, look for these in practice and develop a clear idea about how these are helping to achieve the overall goal.

    b. Share the positives with staff during a meeting – be clear to explain how you see these active ingredients improving the target area.

    c. Send an email to all staff with the highlights of the Quality Assurance that week/half-term. Be sure to recognise what you want repeated!

d. Talk to staff. Aim to visit a teacher in each department and ask them how the focus area/system/process feels in their day-to-day practice; ask for feedback: *what would make this even better for you?*

e. If you still teach, ensure you demonstrate the active ingredients consistently – and ask for staff to visit your classroom.

4. **Forming hypotheses**: use your Quality Assurance to make accurate hypotheses and adjust the system/process as necessary. Quality Assurance shouldn't just give you information – it should be a platform to make things better!

   a. Because you have clarity about the active ingredients of the system/process collect the evidence you need to recognise when something isn't working as planned.

   b. Communicate early with staff – this might be in a meeting. Ask for feedback in a way it can be responded to and acted upon. Your teaching and support staff might be relying on the system/process every day – if something isn't working well, they will be key to helping to find a fix!

   c. Adjust – ensuring it is evidence-informed and moulded by your context. Give yourself the time and space necessary to plan the adjustments necessary to the system/process.

   d. Where necessary offer additional training and rehearsal time. If adjustments have been made to the active ingredients, it probably won't be enough to just tell staff – even if they agree with the adjustments. The knowing-doing gap might mean changes are not made to the original model.

   e. Return to the first step – and scrutinise the changes you've made in practice around the school and talk to your staff. *Is this working better for you? Have the changes improved the system/process?*

5. **Ensure the members of staff who are Quality Assuring are consistent and aligned**: If multiple members of staff are Quality Assuring the active ingredients of a system or process, there shouldn't be any breathing space between them. When misalignment exists it creates ambiguity.

   a. Dedicate time with your team to ensure they have clarity about the active ingredients – both examples and nonexamples. The team should understand what this system/process is hoping to achieve. Create a strong shared mental model.

   b. Complete joint Quality Assurance with your team visits and ask questions to gauge awareness and strengthen their mental model.

   c. Set Quality Assurance as a consistent agenda item and ask your team to summarise what they've seen. This will both hold staff to account to do the Quality Assurance and will provide you with useful information on the system/process – as well as their perception and awareness.

d. Link with another school (perhaps within your Multi Academy Trust – or a partner school) and use a fresh pair of eyes to look for consistency and alignment; this may well reveal blind spots.

e. Check and talk about bias with the team. Bias is natural; make it normal to recognise it and subsequently check it.

References

Didau, D. (2020) *Intelligent Accountability.* John Catt Educational, Limited.

EEF (2024) "A school's guide to implementation guidance report." Education Endowment Foundation, https://educationendowmentfoundation.org.uk/education-evidence/guidance-reports/implementation. Accessed 28 July 2024.

Robinson, V. (2011) *Student-Centered Leadership.* Wiley.

13 Making decisions

What is important?

In *Time to Think*, Rachel Johnson (2023) states that "the people you work with will sense what you stand for by watching your behaviour, your reactions, and your decisions". We believe it is really important to know – and have absolute clarity over – what you stand for; this will guide your decision-making. When you commit to decisions which conflict with what you stand for, you'll likely experience cognitive dissonance. This discomfort is experienced when a person holds conflicting beliefs, attitudes, or values, or when their actions contradict their beliefs. Cognitive dissonance theory suggests that people are motivated to maintain consistency in their thoughts and actions to alleviate this discomfort – when our decisions match what we stand for we avoid the discomfort of cognitive dissonance.

People-pleasing and always trying to gain broad consensus can compromise effective decision-making. Johnson believes that we are people-pleasing when "we are only comfortable making decisions when we are not disliked or rejected" and "we look to others to validate us and the decisions we have made". As school leaders, there will be times when decisions need to be made quickly and confidently – and there will be times when school leaders can slow down and discuss decision-making. School leaders need to be prepared to work in both these ways – to rely too heavily on one way of working will not always yield the best outcome. We recall visiting a head teacher's office and on his printer was the quote "doing what's popular is not always right, and doing what's right is not always popular". We think this is a useful quote when considering the decisions you will make for the school or department. Leaders will never please all the staff – but that does not mean that we shouldn't listen and understand, and even if we choose a different direction, staff will appreciate being heard and understood.

In "How to Make Great Decisions, Quickly", Martin Moore (2022) suggests eight elements that optimise the speed and accuracy of decision-making: (1) great decisions are shaped by consideration of many different viewpoints; (2) great decisions are made as close as possible to the action; (3) great decisions address the root cause, not just the symptoms; (4) great decisions are made by a clearly accountable person; (5) great decisions consider the holistic impacts of a problem; (6) great decisions balance short-term and long-term value; (7) great decisions are communicated well to stakeholders; and (8) great decisions are timely.

School leaders may find it useful to engage with a pre-mortem – a technique used in decision-making and project planning to identify potential failure points or risks before they occur. In a pre-mortem, the team imagines that the project has failed and then works backwards to determine what could have led to that failure. This allows the team to anticipate challenges, vulnerabilities, and pitfalls, enabling them to take proactive measures to mitigate risks and increase the likelihood of project success. Essentially, a pre-mortem helps teams uncover blind spots and address potential issues before they become serious problems.

In *Clear Thinking* Shane Parish (2024) warns his readers to guard against and be aware of the four main instincts that represent our brain's default: the Emotional Default: we respond to feelings rather than reason. The Ego Default: we react to things that attack our self-worth. The Social Default: we try to conform to the norms of the group. The Inertia Default: we favour habits and comfort rather than change. When driven blindly by one of these instincts, it can lead to poor decision-making. In busy organisations it is not surprising that leaders can occasionally make decisions that are not ideal.

Be careful not to act on emotions in the heat of a situation; it can be easy to react emotionally to incidents when they occur at school during an already stressful day. Careful thought, consideration, and communication with senior leaders, school staff, children, and parents are essential when enacting major change – these changes are not made during a hectic, busy, emotional day.

Parish goes on to suggest that to avoid making a choice rather than making an informed decision, leaders can follow four deliberate stages: define the problem, explore tentative solutions, evaluate said options, and choose the best one. School leaders should consider opportunity cost, which refers to the value of the next best alternative that is foregone when a decision is made. In other words, it's the cost of choosing one option over another, taking into account the benefits that could have been gained from the alternative option. Understanding opportunity cost helps school leaders make more informed decisions by considering the trade-offs involved in their choices. Parish suggests leaders would benefit from the "3-Lens Principle" when viewing opportunity cost: first, compared with what? Two, and then what? Three, at the expense of what?

> **KEY TAKEAWAYS**
>
> - When leaders make decisions which match what they stand for, they avoid the discomfort of cognitive dissonance.
> - Leaders can be influenced – both consciously and subconsciously – by bias and defaults.
> - Leaders could utilise the "3-Lens Principle" as a tool to consider opportunity cost.

Elliot would often attend senior leadership meetings in his previous school and the headteacher would simply list what the school was going to do with little if any discussion, very much one person's viewpoint. Elliot felt this de-skilled him and reduced the autonomy to develop areas within his portfolio. This was not the style Elliot wished to use; he remembered once being told by his mentor that his most important task was not to arrive at the meeting with all the answers but to leave the meeting with the answers, listen to all the voices, they will see things he couldn't from a range of different viewpoints. Ultimately he made the call, but it was made on what was best for the school and what he aligned with. Members of his senior team appreciated being heard, even if Elliot didn't always follow their suggestions.

Elliot made sure that he didn't simply replicate decisions from his past leadership experiences, which would be too comfortable and ultimately not always correct for a school in a different community.

Amara was confident that the departments were improving, and the robust quality assurance procedures confirmed this. She had ensured that when the departments discussed symptoms that caused issues she unpicked it with her team to find what the root cause might be; she looked up the stream as opposed to down it. Historically the department had spent hours talking over symptoms, late arrival of equipment, timetabling issues, and use of IT to share resources. The department now took each symptom and systematically worked out what the root cause might be. Then they took action to ensure it could be improved. Discussions with the finance and purchasing departments, input into the timetable whilst it was being formed, not just small tweaks at the end, how best to use IT for sharing of resources with experts. Each decision made the department better; every small step made working in the department more enjoyable. It was like the departments became detectives, breaking each symptom down to its root cause (Figure 13.1).

Marco hugely enjoyed leading on behaviour; he knew others in the school wouldn't want his portfolio area but he was all in. He often came across challenges from his own staff, and he welcomed and encouraged this. Marco stuck with his beliefs. Over his time developing behaviour he had been challenged by the community on social media and parents shouting in reception – he had been under pressure to change and move away from what he believed, but he stood firm with the staff at the school. Whilst staff challenged him he knew the school stood together on the decisions he made. Marco could have bent and taken the easier road of people-pleasing those that shouted the loudest, but inside he knew the decisions the school made improved lives, especially those pupils from the most disadvantaged backgrounds.

With this in mind, what purposeful steps can Elliot, Amara, and Marco take – and other leaders in similar positions – to make great decisions?

Figure 13.1 Making decisions – Amara.

1. **Reversible and irreversible decisions**: Jeff Bezos, the founder of Amazon, asks himself: is this a reversible or irreversible decision?

    a. Decide whether the decision you need to make is reversible or irreversible – meaning, can it be undone or changed, or is it permanent?

    b. If your decision is reversible, you can use your domain-specific knowledge to make faster decisions. Not every decision you make as a leader requires you to gather as much information as possible or collect other perspectives. If you're facing a reversible decision you can make quick decisions and avoid decision-paralysis.

    c. Reversible decisions can still be valuable: view them as opportunities to teach you more, quicker because they are reversible. Reflect on the decision made and the impact it has had.

    d. If your decision is irreversible, your thinking will need to be slower and more deliberate. Consider: how much would it cost (in time, money, goodwill, etc.) to undo – this will inform you how far down the irreversible continuum it is.

   e. Irreversible decisions should be made as late as possible – you may wish to use a decision-making tool to help you gather the information you need to make an informed decision.

2. **There is a tendency to stop thinking when we think we're right**: This can hamper good decision-making. The Ladder of inference (developed by the American Chris Argyris, a former professor at Harvard Business School, in 1970) can help leaders actively avoid cognitive biases.

   a. Look for all available data – and select what is useful. Consider: what data have you chosen to ignore or disregard?

   b. Analyse how you are interpreting the data: what assumptions have you made? Do they stand up to scrutiny? Why are you interpreting the current reality the way you are?

   c. Arrive at an informed conclusion and question: why did you conclude this? Are the conclusions based on reliable evidence from all available data?

   d. As you move closer to a decision, reflect on your own beliefs: what beliefs are guiding your decision-making? What do you believe and why? Where did it come from?

   e. Decide what best action should be taken – why do you believe this is the right action to take? What are the alternatives?

3. **A pre-mortem (developed by Gary Klein) engineers prospective hindsight and can help leaders at all levels make the right decisions to ensure actions are successful**: A pre-mortem is best undertaken with a team to gain collective intelligence towards better decision-making.

   a. Prepare enough information about the project and the decisions you have made in order for the team to understand your thinking and proposed actions.

   b. Tap into the profound power of story-telling: have your audience believe that failure *has* happened – that you are a month or a year post-project and the decisions you made have led to disastrous failure. Make it compelling and vivid.

   c. Generate reasons for failure: ask the team to consider reasons for this epic failure. This is best done individually – give the team two minutes to bullet point as many reasons for failure as possible.

d. Collect the reasons: you could do this by giving each member of the team 60 seconds to share their reasons and collate the reasons visibly (on a flipchart) so that everyone can see patterns and rhythm.

e. Revisit your original plan: return to the here and now – how could you make better decisions to avoid possible future failure?

4. **Sunk cost fallacy**: the sunk cost fallacy refers to the inclination to persist in a task or course of action, even when stopping would be more advantageous. This occurs because we have already committed time, energy, or other resources and feel that quitting would render those investments futile.

    a. Gather information to help you objectively decide whether your decision or action is working. Actively guard against evaluating the impact in isolation – your cognitive bias might obscure reality.

    b. Consider how influential the Ego Default is on your decision-making: are you persisting with a decision or action in order to promote or protect your self-image? If this was your decision, are you worried about what your colleagues will think of you if you choose to abandon it?

    c. The Emotional Default can hinder your ability to make decisions rationally. Scrutinise your thinking and decision-making – particularly at times of high stress or if you haven't had enough sleep. Become consciously aware of how you're feeling and how these feelings are feeding into your decision-making.

    d. Look back: one of the best ways to decide whether a decision is worth persisting with is learning from the past. If success has been limited or halting up until now, things are unlikely to get better without significant change.

    e. Look forwards: once you've looked back at the path you've already taken, you need to consider where you're going and whether the decisions you're making are going to get you there. If the future feels brighter and more successful if you make a change, then cut your losses and let it go.

5. **Opportunity cost**: when making a decision, it is crucial to consider what you might forfeit by not selecting an alternative option.

    a. Carefully define the problem you're looking to solve: guard against identifying the symptoms of the problem and not identifying the problem itself.

    b. Create a list or flowchart of the possible decisions: you may choose to ask others to contribute to this.

    c. Consider "then what?": think about a snapshot picture of where each decision will lead – what will it give you? What are the potential gains?

d. Consider "at the expense of what?": what becomes difficult (or impossible)? Determine the potential losses if you choose your preferred decision.

   e. Make your informed decision: select the option that presents the greatest opportunities and appears to be the most beneficial for you or the company.

References

Johnson, R. (2023) *Time to Think*. John Catt.
Moore, Martin G. (2022) "How to make great decisions, quickly." *Harvard Business Review*, https://hbr.org/2022/03/how-to-make-great-decisions-quickly. Accessed 10 March 2024.
Parish, S. (2024) *Clear Thinking*. Random House UK Limited.

14 Wellbeing

What is important?

We understand that ensuring staff's wellbeing is a priority that leads to improved job performance and lower levels of employee burn-out. From our experience, we think that the only sustainable and truly effective way to manage your staff's wellbeing is getting the environment in which they work right. If the environment in which your staff operate is characterised by high stress and high workload, then being treated to a pastry once every six weeks will be futile. In the "State of education 2023: workload and wellbeing", the National Education Union (NEU) reveals that "almost half of teachers working in England and Wales (48%) view their workload as "unmanageable", to one degree or another. A third (34%) are on the borderline of "only just manageable". With the issue of staff recruitment in countries across the world, looking after the staff we have could not be more important for leaders. That said, looking after our school leaders is also vital to have a healthy organisation. If we are not looking after ourselves and our own health we have little chance of supporting others. Coaching, counselling, and mentoring can all help.

In *Time to Think*, Rachael Johnson (2023) suggests that "when we are tired, stressed, overwhelmed, and under pressure we are generally not at our best". At any time in schools, there will be staff feeling a combination of these inhibitors that will be undermining their performance in the classroom, in the corridors, on the phone to parents, in meetings. School leaders will, of course, also be feeling these things. Johnson believes that "if we are able to have honest conversations well, model boundaries, really listen to people and be clear so that we reduce confusion" then we can be at our best more of the time. Johnson also proposes that fostering a sense of belonging at work is important to our mental health and well-being and creates fulfilment. More than a pain au raisin ever will.

In *The Power of Teams*, Sam Crome suggests that "staff need to feel a sense of agency over how they do their work, their workload, their training and development opportunities, and how much they are trusted". We believe that school Trusts need to be aware of the over-centralisation of schools. Whilst health and safety, finance, and human resources, for example, may become centralised, be aware of removing staff autonomy and removing staff agency. It could be that we lose our most agile and creative staff if they feel restricted. Whilst the short-term benefits of over-centralisation may be beneficial, the longer-term picture could be quite the opposite. Of course, that is not to say this couldn't happen in a single school, it could.

Crome suggests that "wellbeing is an endeavour without an end, but one that will pay dividends in staff morale effectiveness and retention".

> **KEY TAKEAWAYS**
>
> - Ensuring staff well-being requires creating a supportive work environment, as high stress and workload cannot be offset by occasional treats.
> - School leaders must also prioritise their own well-being to effectively support their staff, using tools like coaching and mentoring.
> - Staff need a sense of control over their work and development opportunities. Over-centralisation can stifle creativity and reduce morale.

Elliot understood the recruitment crisis facing schools in many countries. He wanted the best teachers and leaders at his schools but also knows that leafy suburbs can be linked with better outcomes, and this can be attractive to school staff. He also knows that if he could pay his staff an extra allowance to work at his school it's a short-term plan and he doesn't believe long term that is what keeps staff happy (and he cannot afford it!). He knows that staff wellbeing should be high on his list of priorities if he is to employ and retain the best staff – these are his co-workers and he wants them to be happy and healthy.

Once again he reaches out to his staff. Elliot is a high-performing school leader but he knows he doesn't have all the answers (perhaps that is why he is successful). Elliot sets up a workload group at the school to ensure that the areas the staff spend time on are what is most effective. In his previous role as deputy head he used to see staff walking out with boxes of books to mark each evening and was then not surprised that within a few short years they left the profession, did marking those books make more of a difference than the great teacher the profession lost? Staff set up an electronic wellbeing wall and added activities and events and links to useful resources. The staff began to grow their own plans for improving wellbeing and would arrive with suggestions. Staff understood that Elliot valued them and would listen and act. The school had a culture of wellbeing; it was difficult to write it down as a policy but you could feel it.

Amara was proud of the staff she led and had developed professional development opportunities that provided the teachers with a degree of autonomy and self-choice over areas they wished to develop. This was a positive move from the one-size-fits-all approach of previous leaders.

However, she had a nagging doubt over how her support staff were feeling valued. It appeared to Amara that unless you were a teacher very little professional development was planned and quality assured. She spoke with the technicians and teaching assistants and the message was clear; they felt undervalued when the topic of professional development was discussed. This caused issues with wellbeing and often they would leave so they could develop outside of the school.

Amara put plans in place to ensure that the development of support staff was as highly regarded as that of their teacher colleagues. It was revolutionary, and support staff fully engaged with the process and often would want to discuss how they had been learning and improving. The system spreads to other departments until it became a full school policy with catering, premises, office, and all staff linked to the school involved. Staff satisfaction improves from the quality assurance surveys conducted.

Marco knows that for staff well-being the most important element he can provide is a calm, safe, and respectful working environment. The staff voice is clear on this. Calm, orderly classrooms where teachers can teach and children can learn are imperative to staff wellbeing. That is why he stays true to his beliefs, does not bend under pressure, and regularly takes staff feedback. He ensures that there is no disconnect between what the senior leadership say about behaviour and what the staff at the chalkface say, he doesn't hide away and blame teachers if a disconnect appears, and he finds the root cause and works diligently to fix it (Figure 14.1).

As a result the school that Marco works at retains and attracts the very best staff; when adverts for positions are advertised (and that's rare) staff from local schools apply. The school serves a disadvantaged community but they are attracting the most effective teachers, nothing could be more important.

With this in mind, what purposeful steps can Elliot, Amara, and Marco take – and other leaders in similar positions – to support their own and others' wellbeing?

Figure 14.1 Well-being – Marco

1. **Looking after your own wellbeing**: if you are suffering from stress and anxiety as a leader what should you do? It's important to build yourself a support system and not suffer alone. An empty cup cannot fill another.
    a. Find a regular space to talk over the challenges you are facing with a mentor or coach: talking over your challenges can be very beneficial. Fortunately, in today's workplace finding space to talk is much more usual and valued. If you are struggling, reach out to your line manager, occupational health team, or your human resource advisor.
    b. Build in time during the day for positive conversations: as a school leader the day can quickly become busy with challenging conversations. Finding a time to visit a class and listen to children read for example can quickly recentre your day and remind why you took on this position. In our experience we always kept the last hour on a Friday free to visit classes and speak with children – we never had a pre-planned meeting allocated to this time unless absolutely necessary. Often we would read to a small group of children in the library – it was a joyful way to end each week.
    c. Can you access a trained counsellor to talk over your anxiety? Some countries and districts now employ staff counsellors on a full-time basis to support leaders and staff. We have experienced this and the support for staff was invaluable. For some leaders a school chaplain can offer support. External services are also available online and leaders can quickly connect with trained psychological practitioners and therapists via a phone call or self-referral. In England, Scotland, and Wales the NHS 111 number currently offers a mental health option if you are in crisis.
    d. Ensure you have time to reflect: these moments can be very beneficial. As leaders we often just want to press on but reflection is vital. Find time to stop and recognise your achievements. When discussing the development plan ensure you build in time to reflect on all that you have achieved and not simply press on without the recognition you (and your team) deserve.
    e. Take exercise: often new leaders ignore their physical fitness and that impacts on them. We have experience of leaders no longer having the time to exercise or eat healthy. Regular exercise contributes to a healthier and happier life. Other benefits of exercise include:
        i. boosting our self-esteem and confidence
        ii. increasing motivation and focus
        iii. reducing tension, anxiety, stress and mental fatigue
        iv. helping to calm the mind, especially when dealing with difficult emotions like anger, frustration and sadness

> v. reducing loneliness by offering new ways to get together with family and friends and meet new people
>
> (NHS – Every mind Matters, 2024)

2. **Research shows that high-demand jobs with low job resources can lead to burn-out** (Bakker and Costa, 2014). Education can sit firmly in this category. As a leader how can you reduce burn-out amongst your staff?

    a. What sense of autonomy do your staff have? Do different staff have different levels, e.g. administration staff/teachers? Can you review what levels of autonomy staff believe they have and could this lead to any potential changes? Do the changes you make at the school/department/pastoral team impact on staff autonomy – make this part of your thinking when creating change. It's important.

    b. Provide staff feedback on the work they are completing: have you considered how often you provide staff feedback? Have you asked staff how often and what type of feedback they would value? Don't leave this until staff appraisal if your school conducts this infrequently during the academic year, e.g. for staff performance management two or three times a year. Add staff feedback to your regular line management sessions if possible. If not, have you considered how you provide feedback to your department staff or primary leads? Find space and plan this out at the beginning of the year so everyone has clarity on when it happens.

    c. Know your staff: staff need to have high levels of trust with their line manager to be open about their personal well-being. This allows genuine connections to occur. Referrals to occupational health should be considered and this should always be in your mind when discussing issues of wellbeing with your team. Make sure you share details of support available to staff. Be aware of your staff's ways of working and working patterns – for example staff that are perfectionists can be overly critical of themselves and this can lead them to anxiety and depression (Blatt, 1995). Staff that send emails late into the evening or early morning might need further support. Always speak with your human resource link for advice.

    d. Ensure that new staff have time to build relationships and feel part of the team: if possible, allocate an extra space on the timetable for new staff to meet on regular occasions so they can learn and gain support from each other. It might cost the school an hour a fortnight of a teacher but we believe the benefits will outweigh the cost. Don't simply assume that new staff will become part of the team.

    e. Work can contribute to a meaningful life: if staff feel their work is meaningful they experience higher well-being (Ward and King, 2017). When staff don't feel their work is meaningful it is often because they just see their own individual tasks in isolation. Ensure that all your staff understand and can visualise the goal of the school and how the tasks they undertake contribute to achieving it. When President John Kennedy visited NASA and came across a cleaner, he asked him what his job was and the cleaner replied: "My job is to help put a man on the moon". This shows the complete staff alignment with the aims of the organisation.

3. **It is often the small things that we do at school that can contribute to staff well-being:** we have experience of schools running various initiatives that have contributed to an increased feeling of staff well-being.

   a. Staff receiving a postcard of thanks from the leadership team in the post: at schools we have seen these given out as part of a thank you Friday at staff briefings but it's hard to acknowledge all the good work of a school each week and staff can feel left out. A card posted home to arrive on a Saturday morning can be a great start to the weekend.

   b. Use one of your middle leaders meeting at the end of a term for a session of thanks: allocate each middle leader to a colleague in the room and ask them to write a card of thanks to be read out at the meeting. These can be powerful and personal.

   c. Involve all the children in a staff "thank you" day: we have experience of staff arriving at school being greeted by banners of thanks and food prepared by the students. Short notes of gratitude were then distributed to staff during the day and even staff cars being cleaned!

   d. Bring staff together: by organising events such as staff sports events or time for a Friday coffee and cake. We always worry when the biscuits for senior leader meetings are better than for staff ones! Remember, we are all co-workers.

   e. Find a physical space for all staff to meet and talk: it appears that in some newly built schools staffrooms are being removed. This can lead to staff believing they are not trusted to be together and can impact on trust.

4. **Staff relationships** are the most important element to develop and maintain to secure staff well-being – but how is this done?

   a. Ensure that even on busy days, you acknowledge each member of staff that you pass. A simple hello with their name can mean a great deal. Remember, as a leader you leave a wake behind you.

   b. Listen to your staff: you do not need to agree with them but give them time to explain their thoughts on the school with you. They will respect you for listening.

c. When you arrive at the school: say hello to the kitchen staff and premises staff and anyone else who might already be in school.

d. Show humility and vulnerability with your co-workers: it can be that a lack of confidence restricts leaders from doing this. Actually, the more experienced the leader, the more often this happens in our experience (Section 1, Chapter 2: *Vulnerability* will provide you with the steps to achieve this).

e. Show compassion for your staff: high performance and high compassion are not mutually exclusive. Many of the very best leaders we have worked with show compassion to their staff – they understand that their co-workers are not simply commodities. Are there times when you allow a member of staff to attend their child's first performance in a play or cover a member of staff's class that might be struggling to keep up to date with reports due to issues outside school? Staff will undoubtedly pay this back with their discretionary effort.

5. **Think of how the actions of senior leaders impact on the staff wellbeing**: Be strong and stay loyal to your beliefs, even under pressure from external factors.

    a. If you arrange a staff meeting ensure staff have the time for any pre-reading that is required. It's too easy to expect it to be done 24 hours before an event and this inevitably eats into the staff's personal life or removes what they had planned in this time. Always consider the member of staff with a full teaching commitment or the early career teacher planning away from school.

    b. Micromanagement by senior leaders can lead to increased stress for your staff. Consider what management you need to complete and if this aids the school's leadership and performance.

    c. Invest in your co-workers' careers – use your expert staff or links outside of your organisation to achieve this, even in times of financial constraints. How can you use time within contracted 1,265 hours (England) to fit in career development?

    d. Leaders should nurture a caring culture at the school by being the ones to promote it. If you are sending emails late in the evening or over the weekend, question how is this helping your staff? A word of warning…the idea we can send emails outside of working hours and tell staff that they don't need to open them doesn't work – if necessary send the emails on a timed send. Use your emotional intelligence to show you care – we have known school leaders never ask a staff member how they are after a family member passed away; please don't let this be you.

e. Act upon the concerns that are raised with you; don't simply squash them down because you are fearful of ground truths. It is not the job of leaders to cut off staff concerns for fear of reprisals from leaders. Feedback is a gift – use it to promote well-being with staff genuinely being listened to.

References

Bakker, A. B. and Costa, P. L. (2014) Chronic job burnout and daily functioning: A theoretical analysis. *Burnout Research*, 1(3), 112–119.

Blatt, S. J. (1995) The destructiveness of perfectionism. *American Psychologist*, 50(12), 1003–1020.

Crome, S. (2023) *The Power of Teams: How to Create and Lead Thriving School Teams*. John Catt.

Johnson, R. (2023) *Time to Think*. John Catt.

NEU (2023) "State of education 2023: Workload and wellbeing." National Education Union, neu.org.uk. Accessed 28 July 2024.

NHS (2024) "Be active for your mental health." Every Mind Matters – NHS, www.nhs.uk. Accessed 4th August 2024.

Ward, S. J. and King, L. A. (2017) Work and the good life: How work contributes to a meaningful life. *Research in Organisational Behaviour*, 37, 59–82.

Conclusion

We'd like to thank you for engaging with our book so meaningfully. We absolutely believe that better is possible – regardless of the starting point. We appreciate that leaders' time is limited and really precious and we hugely value that you have given our book some of that time.

Whilst writing this book we often thought about what it was that we would have valued reading before and during our leadership journey. We hope that our combined leadership experience of 40 years helps us to help you.

The time we have spent on this book is dedicated to our current and future school leaders.

Our Probletunity Group

Staff member(s): _____

Problem/Issue/Concern/Frustration:

Opportunity/Solution/Idea/Suggestion:

Sightline Presentation

Sightline presentations

1. What's your problem of practice?

Closing the loop

1. What did you do?
2. How did you inspect what you expect?
3. What were your successes?
4. What were your challenges?

Opening the sightline process (times are maximum – 17 minutes)

5 minutes: Present sightline information for your portfolio area.

3 minutes: Clarifying questions from group. *No advice or discussion, simply a question.*

3 minutes: Presenter to respond to questions and provide any further information.

4 minutes: Advice or feedback to be provided from the group.

2 minutes: Presenter to respond to actions to be taken (what *will* you do?).

Closing the loop process (times are maximum – 5 minutes)

3 minutes: Remind people of sightline key points.

1. What did you do?

2. What were your successes?

3. What were your challenges?

1 minute: Questions/comments from the group.

1 minute: Respond to comments from the field.

Index

Note: **Bold** page numbers refer to tables and *italic* page numbers refer to figures.

above the line behaviours 4, 8
accountability 38–46, *42*; encourage at all levels 44; feedback 38–41, 43, 45; leaders and 38; levels of 43; mechanisms 45–46; negative view of 42; practise 44–45; talk about 43; think about 42–43
accuracy, of decision-making 105
adaptability 47–55, *51*; debrief 54–55; feedback 55; keep your emotions in check 52–53; to respond to need 54; situational awareness development 53; think about leadership styles 51–52
adaptive decision-making: team management 80
The Advantage (Lencioni) 15, 24
affiliative leaders 47
alignment 24, 31, 57, 80, 91, 94, 116
All Blacks 56
alliances 78, 79
Ambition Institute 25
artefacts 59
attendance 33, 37, 46, 56
authoritative (visionary) leaders 47
autonomy 17, 28, 35, 40, 48, 54, 97, 98, 106, 112, 115

behaviour 28, 31, 40–42, 44–46, 48, 58, 92, 98, 99, 104, 106; change 3, 8, 90; goal-oriented 53; for learning model 50; at school 17, 27, 68; *see also individual entries*

below the line behaviours 4, 8
betrayal 3, 5, 7, 8
Bezos, Jeff 107
blogs 69, 85
body language 11, 41
Botherdness (Roberts) 75
Brown, Brene 14, 39, 83; *Dare to Lead* 4, 13
Buck, Andy 48; *Leadership Matters* 47
Building Culture (Sharma) 31, 39, 82
building trust 7, 9, 11
bypass model 90, *91*

Carucci, Ron 38
causal reasoning 52, 64
celebration: clarity 36; Quality Assurance 101–102; vision 30
change management 90–96, *93*; "hurrying slowly" approach 96; model for 95; prioritising 93–94; staff involvement 95–96; understanding 94
change, priorities of 93–94
clarity 31–37, *34*; celebrate wins 36; codification 35–36; communicating with 34–35; of communication 32; creation 31; of culture 31; feedback 32; seeking clarification 35; sightline process 36–37
coaching leaders 47
codification, clarity 35–36
codified behaviour 36
Coe, Rob 15

cognitive dissonance theory 52, 104
Cole, Mark 25
collective intelligence 22, 48, 50, 88
communication 101; clarity of 32; effective 78, 101; frequency 32; open 47, 67, 80; school 59
compassion 4, 66, 117
conductor *vs.* leadership 1
conflict: management of healthy conflict 20–21; swift conflict resolution 79
Continuing Professional Development (CPD) 71, 82
Covey, Stephen 3
Coyle, Daniel 3, 10, 14, 19, 43, 70; *The Culture Code* 3, 13, 31; *The Culture Playbook* 4
Crome, Sam 20, 112; *The Power of Teams* 32, 82; *The Power of Teams* 111
culture/cultural: clarity of 31; legacy 59; Quality Assurance 100–101; scripts 66
The Culture Code (Coyle) 3, 13, 31
The Culture Playbook (Coyle) 4
curriculum planning 45

Dare to Lead (Brown) 4, 13
debrief: accountability 45; adaptability 54–55
decision-making 104–110, *107*; opportunity cost 109–110; pre-mortem 108–109; reversible and irreversible decisions 107–108; speed and accuracy of 105; sunk cost fallacy 109; tendency to stop thinking 108
deficit model, school leadership 98
Delgado, Jennfier 49
democratic leaders 48, 50
development plan 29, 60, 62, 91, 92, 99, 114
Didau, David: *Intelligent Accountability* 39, 98
directive leaders 48
directive leadership approach 50, 54
dissatisfaction 48, 90
domain-specific knowledge 1, 63, 65, 107
Dusting off Thunderbolts (Jones) 1

Edmondson, Amy: *The Right Kind of Wrong* 83
Education Endowment Foundation (EEF) 98–99
effective communication 78, 91
effective leadership 61, 91
Ego Default 105, 109
embrace silence 11
Emotional Default 105, 109
emotional intelligence 51, 76
enactment 59, 79
engagement model 90–91
Evans, Matthew 90; *Leaders with Substance* 66
evidence-based approach 85, 94
exercise 91, 114–115

feedback 118; accountability 38–41, 43, 45; adaptability 55; clarity 32; finding your voice 66–68, 72; loops 82–83, 87–88; Quality Assurance 102; team development 82–84, 87, 88; trust 4; vision 30; vulnerability 18, 19, 22; wellbeing 115, 118
fierce accountability 39
Fierce Conversations (Scott) 3
Fierce Leadership (Scott) 14, 39
finding your voice 65–74, *68*; with angry parents 73–74; delivering to parents/assembly/CPD 71–72; everyone has voice 69–71; feedback 66–68, 72; as lever for change 69; preparing for online meeting 72–73
floodlight leadership behaviours 1, 2
Flores, Fernando 3, 7, 8
follow-up 43, 44, 79
freedom 7, 17, 51, 61

Gavin, Matt: "Leadership *vs.* Management: What's the Difference?" 76
Goleman, Daniel 48; *Leadership That Gets Results* 47
Goyder, Caroline 71
group cooperation 13

healthy organisation 1, 31, 38, 111
Heath, Dan: *Upstream* 82, 83
high-demand jobs with low job resources 115–116; wellbeing 115–116
hope: adaptability 48; legacy 56, 62; vision 29
Hopeful Schools (Myatt) 56
human map 78
"hurrying slowly" approach 93
hypotheses, Quality Assurance 102

identification, team management 79
Inertia Default 105
intelligent accountability 39, 45
Intelligent Accountability (Didau) 39, 98
internal politics, team management 78–79
irreversible decisions 107–108

Jacobson, Brown 73
Johnson, Rachel: *Time to Think* 39, 56, 65, 104, 111
Jones, Sir John: *Dusting off Thunderbolts* 1
judgement 7, 51–52

Kennedy, John 116
Kerr, James 10; *Legacy* 14, 56
Kneebone, Roger 64
knowledge sharing 32
Kotter, John 91

Ladder of inference 108
Lane, C. 38
leaders 47; and accountability 42, 43; pre-mortem 108–109
Leaders Eat Last (Sinek) 25, 76
leadership 1, 24–25, 44, 69, 76, 97; adaptability 52, 54; behaviour 1, 13, 14, 83; development 61, 86; educational 80; floodlight 1–2, *2*; habit 19, 43; model *2*, 63, *63*; patience as 29; quality of 25, 82; in schools 97, 98, 100, 117; styles 47–51, 53–55; team 24, 31, 36, 38, 39, 57, 65, 116; vulnerability in 15, 22
Leadership for Teacher Learning (Wiliam) 48
Leadership Matters (Buck) 47

Leadership Plain and Simple (Radcliffe) 57–58
leadership styles 47, 48, 50; keep your emotions in check 52–53; situational awareness development 53; think about 51–52
Leadership That Gets Results (Goleman) 47
"Leadership vs. Management: What's the Difference?" (Gavin) 76
Leaders with Substance (Evans) 66
Leading with Vulnerability (Morgan) 15
learning 16, 17, 22, 34, 35, 38, 40, 41, 45, 47, 48, 50, 82, 85–88, 97–99, 109, 113
legacy 56–62, *58*; cultivating right environment 60–61; culture 59; hope 62; leadership development 61
Legacy (Kerr) 14, 56
Lencioni, Patrick 21, 28, 31, 38; *The Advantage* 15, 24
lesson visits 45, 79, 97
line behaviours 4, 8
Line Management: meeting 16, 67; systems 45
listening 3, 11, 73, 116; overcommunicate your listening 3, 11–12, 31, 44

management 76; demand 80; leadership and 76; staff performance 115; *see also* change management; team management
Maxwell, John 25; *The 21 Indispensable Qualities of a Leader–Becoming a Person Others Will Want to Follow* 25
mental scripts 66
micromanagement 117
Mindful S.N.A.C.K. (STOP NOTICE ACCEPT CURIOUS KINDNESS) 52–53
Moldoveanu, M.: "The power of predictability" 76
Moore, Martin 105
Morgan, Jacob 20; *Leading with Vulnerability* 15
muscular humility 10–11
Myatt, Mary: *Hopeful Schools* 56

National Education Union (NEU) 111
Naumburg, Carla 52–53
"The Neuroscience of Trust" (Zak) 4
neuroscience research 4

online websites 85
open communication 47, 78, 80; channels 67
opportunity cost 109–110
organisations 1, 3–5, 8–11, 13–16, 18, 22, 24, 25, 28, 30, 31, 36, 42–44, 47, 48, 50, 55, 56, 59, 61, 62, 65–67, 76, 78, 91, 95, 105, 111, 116, 117
overcommunicate your listening 3, 11–12, 31, 44

pacesetting leaders 48, 54
Parish, Shane: *Clear Thinking* 105
peer-to-peer accountability 38–39
'The People Business' 1
people-pleasing 39, 104, 107
phronesis 75
Polzer, Jeff 13
positive conversations 114
"The power of predictability" (Stevenson and Moldoveanu) 76
The Power of Teams (Crome) 32, 82, 111
predictability, team management 79–80
predictive processing framework 80
pre-mortem 105; decision-making 108–109
"Primal Leadership" 48
problem talk 91
Probletunity Group creation 44
professional development opportunities 85
professionalism 73, 79
professional learning 82, 88
psychologically safe environment, vulnerability 18–20
psychological safety 15, 98

Quality Assurance 97–103, *100*; celebration 101–102; culture 100–101; ensure staff members 102–103; feedback 102; high-demand jobs with low job resources 115–116; hypotheses 102; senior leaders impact 117–118; staff relationships 116–117; staff well-being 116; understanding 101

Radcliffe, Steve: *Leadership Plain and Simple* 57–58
Radical Candour (Scott) 4
Reduce Change to Increase Improvement (Robinson) 90, 98
reflection 4, 10, 25, 39, 51, 54, 55, 80, 107, 108, 114
reframe internal politics 79
research-based institute 86–87
response 3, 19, 31, 38, 49, 79, 80, 88
reversible decisions 107–108
The Right Kind of Wrong (Edmondson) 83
Roberts, Hywel: *Botherdness* 75
Robinson, Vivian 91, 96; *Reduce Change to Increase Improvement* 90, 98

schemas/patterns 52
school(s): codifying practice in 35; culture 59; development plan 91; leadership in 97; staff well-being at 116; vision for 25–26, 28, 30
"School Environment and Leadership: Evidence Review" 15
school leaders 14, 15, 24, 31, 32, 48, 49, 51, 53, 54, 56, 75, 98; accountability 45; challenge for 25; change management 90; decision-making 104, 105; domain-specific knowledge 63; finding your voice 65, 67; pace of innovation 85; prioritising change 93–94; team management 76; vision 25; well-being 111, 114
school leadership 49, 100; deficit model 98; models 98
Schweitzer, Albert 69
Scott, Kim: *Radical Candour* 4
Scott, Susan 15; *Fierce Conversations* 3; *Fierce Leadership* 14, 39
self-accountability 42
self-trust 8
senior leaders 9, 18, 36, 44, 46, 61, 62, 91, 98, 116–118; clarity 36; decision making 105; impact on Quality Assurance 98, 117–118; impact on staff wellbeing 117–118; legacy 61, 62
senior leadership 5, 16, 17, 27, 33
senior leadership teams 41, 45, 65, 67, 76, 84, 86, 100, 106, 113

sharing and embracing failure, vulnerability 21–22
Sharma, Lekha: *Building Culture* 31, 39, 82
sightlines 18, 33, 37; clarity 36–37
Sinek, Simon: *Leaders Eat Last* 25, 76; *Start with Why* 24, 25
situational awareness 49, 54; development 53
Social Default 105
social media 69, 77, 85, 92, 106
social norms 31, 32
Solomon, Robert C. 3, 7, 8
solution-focused coaching 40
speed, of decision-making 105
The Speed of Trust 3
staff: feedback 113, 115; involvement, change management 95–96
staff relationships 116–117; Quality Assurance 116–117; wellbeing 116–117
staff well-being 112, 113, 116, 117; at school 116; senior leaders impact on 117–118
stakeholders: change management 91, 94; clarity 36; decision-making 105; legacy 60; vision 24, 25, 28, 30
Start with Why (Sinek) 24, 25
Stevenson, H.: "The power of predictability" 76
strategic and visionary: team management 78
succession planning 61
sunk cost fallacy 109
surplus model, school leadership 98
sweeping the sheds concept 10–11
swift conflict resolution, team management 79
systematic decision-making process 79

talk and think: about accountability 42; about trust 8
team development 82–88, *84*; feedback 82–84, 87, 88; feedback loops 87–88; leaders set tone for school 86; pace of innovation 85; research-based institute 86–87; stand on balcony 88

team management 75–80, *77*; adaptive decision-making 80; navigating internal politics 78–79; predictability 79–80; strategic and visionary 78; swift conflict resolution 79
think about: accountability 42–43; adaptability 51–52; trust 7–8; vision 28
"3-Lens Principle" 105
Time to Think (Johnson) 39, 56, 65, 104
torchlight behaviours *63*, 63–64
trust 3–12, *7*; an emotional practice 3, 7; build relationships 10–11; feedback 4; make visible 8–9; think about 7–8; vs control 9–10
The 21 Indispensable Qualities of a Leader–Becoming a Person Others Will Want to Follow (Maxwell) 25

Upstream (Heath) 82, 83

Value Complexity Matrix 93–94
vision 24–30; and alignment 24; behave consistently with 29–30; feedback 30; involve all stakeholders 28; make it visible and celebrate small wins 30; think about 28; tools to achieve 29
vulnerability 13–22, **15**, *17*, 70; create designed space 18; exchanges of 14; feedback 18, 19, 22; in leadership 15; leadership isn't about oversharing 22; leaning into 15; loop 14; manage healthy conflict 20–21; psychologically safe environment 18–20; sharing and embracing failure 21–22

wellbeing 111–118, *113*; feedback 115, 118; high-demand jobs with low job resources 115–116; looking after your own 114–115; senior leaders impact on staff wellbeing 117–118; staff 112, 113, 116, 117; staff relationships 116–117
Wiliam, Dylan 49; *Leadership for Teacher Learning* 48
Willingham, Daniel T. 63

Zak, Paul: "The Neuroscience of Trust" 4

For Product Safety Concerns and Information please contact our EU
representative GPSR@taylorandfrancis.com
Taylor & Francis Verlag GmbH, Kaufingerstraße 24, 80331 München, Germany